The Networker

Ned Iceton

and the

Social Developers' Network

(SDN)

The Networker

Ned Iceton
and the
Social Developers' Network
(SDN)

Contributing Authors

Jo Kijas

Ned Iceton (d.2015)

Jane Dunstan

Terry Widders

John Ducker

John Russell

Sylvia Baker (d.2011)

Ben Leeman (d.2015)

Jean Leeman (d.2014)

Tiyana Maksimovic-Binno

David Purnell

Chris Larkin

Mary Porter

Ray Rauscher

Barbara Hicks

David Crew

Jane Dunstan

Acknowledgement

The *Nuturing Evolutionary Development Inc.* wishes to thank the excellent work of Jo Kijas in designing the format of this biographical project, conducting the interviews, transcribing and compiling the material that forms the basis of this book. Interviews were first conducted during 2006, and since then, Ned and some of the contributing authors, have died.

Contents

Overview

The book provides insight into the development of Ned Iceton's theories, embedded in a history of a network of social developers. The inspiration for the Social Developers' Network and the NED-Net Foundation is based on the following perceptions:

- That the earth and human species face a crisis of survival.
- That we all need to use our potential for inner growth for the benefit of all.
- That citizen involvement must be the primary purpose of our next evolutionary step.
- That we need to participate regularly in retreats and workshops to review our goals and objectives.

According to Ned Iceton, the social developer's style is to offer support to anyone as we confront each other about reality. This involves honesty and trust. Personal development accompanies social development in order that both individuals and communities function effectively. Both cognitive and emotional aspects must be considered. Social development is about "re-ordering our individual and social culture as a prescription for our species' ills".

"Complexity theory, chaos theory and human systems dynamics give us new metaphors by which to explore how best we can develop new tools and remain flexible, adaptable and congruent with reality". Centralised systems will fail and we will have to rebuild. Social Developers workshops have evolved to meet this challenge using group processes. The Network provides personal mentoring to self-motivated people for their role as citizens. Diversity of participants is an important feature of the workshops.

Ned saw himself as a 'cultural therapist'. He was inspired by his mother's efforts as a community developer during the Great Depression when she galvanised the town of Gunnedah NSW to cope. His early experiences as a doctor working in the Northern Territory, the UK and the Sub-Continent gave him confidence to engage with many different people and situations. When he returned to Armidale he made contact with Aboriginal people and farmers and developed workshops of mutual support and action. He shared his learning journey with his wife Joan until she died, and then continued to practice meditation as part of managing himself and recognising the unconscious elements in life. "My object has always been to plug every new understanding into every pre-existing one". In later years the restorative justice/ practice approach became for him an example of achieving emotional learning by being cognitively explicit and turning society away from negativism.

Ned Iceton died on 30 June 2015 and was farewelled at a large funeral gathering in Armidale on 7 July. A later memorial meeting was held in Canberra on 24 October. On both occasions strong tributes were given to the significant impact of Ned's life on many people around Australia. Ned left a Foundation to continue promoting creative social development.

Contributing authors:[1]

Terry Widders took part in the early Aboriginal human relationship workshops arranged by Ned, and since then he and Ned have often shared ideas about life and community. He was excited by the possibility of making change to create adaptive communities, and Ned introduced to him concepts like social development, community and negotiation of relationships.

John Ducker was part of the Inverell farmers group that came together with Ned's help. Called the Bannockburn Conservation Group, they focused on soil erosion problems. "Ned always maintained a very unobtrusive presence. He'd sit at the back of a meeting and not enter into it at all, he'd simply observe. Then later he'd strategize the next steps with the group". The self-help approach made the group very successful in working for change.

John Russell, a social worker, helped Ned in forming the Social Developers' Network (SDN). They found common concern for community development, and John pushed Ned to start workshops that ran for a week, really engaging participants in sharing their work as well as their personal problems.

"Ned did the head work, talked about the theory and looked at the process. I was the one who interrupted when I thought there was a sensitive area".

---

1   The Interviews in this book were done well before Ned Iceton died in mid-2015.

Early workshops had a tendency towards confrontation (possibly owing to dominant male influence), but later ones have become more caring. They have become shorter (4 days) and leadership moves around as different issues emerge. There is a strong emphasis on positive social change. Usually about half the participants have been before, and others are new to the process.

Sylvia Baker moved to Deniliquin NSW in her early married life, and became active in advocating for women's interests particularly in her role on the local council. This led to a passion for community development. Her contact with Ned came through a visit to China that he led for the Social Workers Union, and through her friendship with a local Aboriginal woman who knew of Ned's work on Aboriginal studies. "It was really Ned that gave me the impetus for my local government and community work, because he understood what I was on about at a time when I couldn't articulate it". The SDN workshops gave her new energy to carry on. Ned remained "a staunch ally, confidant, support person, and mentor".

Ben Leeman came from a Dutch background, and was keen to learn about all aspects of religion, sociology and social work. John Russell invited him to a SDN workshop and he became a regular participant. "The sharing of personal experiences, often challenging, and the discussion which generated from their presentation, enriches the workshops and provides food for thought and stimulation for ongoing activism". Feedback was given in a positive and developmental way, encouraging individuals to cope better with uncertainties and frustrations of community work. Through all this, Ned has been a shining example of a person who augments his intellectual ability with emotional intelligence. Ben became involved in publishing the New Community journal which NED-Net helped to fund.

Jean Leeman, Ben's wife, had a social work background. Initially she felt challenged by the emotional temperature of the workshops, but later felt that "people are really supportive". Gender has been an issue at times, with the male perspective queried by the female participants. Jean affirmed the value of taking part as a way to "recharge and get on with what you are doing". She valued especially the Guthega workshops as they were held further away from other places and more immune from the interruptions of daily life. "To me one of the most important things about coming, and that has encouraged me to come, has been the mix of people, their wide experience, their commitment to change and to improving things in the world for people". Ned's networking has been vital in keeping the momentum going. "Ned has a huge integrity as a person. Sometimes Little Ned is the one who needs others to support him, while at other times he's the teacher and leader – it's complex and it's good".

Tiyana Maksimovic-Binno had a traumatic time adjusting to life in Australia as a migrant. She reached out for alternatives to the mainstream, and met Ned at Schumacher's memorial conference. She came to the next SDN workshop to share her project for "an alternative, environmentally and emotionally sustainable and healing urban household-community". She found a lively and supportive group of people. "I was so very happy that there was experiential education at SDN, rather than any authoritarian preaching or teaching that I always had an issue with". She experienced mutual respect and a non-judgmental framework. However she stopped attending workshops, partly because she felt some underlying conflicts were not adequately addressed, partly because the format seemed to lack emotional transparency, and partly because the projects discussed were too remote from her daily life to be relevant. "I appreciated Ned tremendously for having had the honesty and courage to step out of his comfortable social status, position and income as MD to co-found SDN and to keep working through it according to his conviction".

David Purnell was attracted by Ned's "broad approach to the issues of social change and personal change". With a background in public service and university administration, and community involvement in Life Line and Australian Frontier, David saw John and Ned as complementary in running the workshops by contributing different elements. Other participants brought methods like dance, drawing, meditation, drama. "SDN was an independent network with whom to check base, get feedback, and some stimulating thoughts about where you could take things".

Christine Larkin, a social worker and David's partner, saw an article by Ned about working with people in rural communities and was excited by it, and came to a workshop. "What appealed to me in those early days was that it was leading-edge knowledge; things that we might not have heard much about otherwise". Her professional group work was influenced by SDN approaches. The workshops became more flexible in that not all sessions were seen as 'compulsory'. In other ways there has been less creativity and this has disappointed Chris. She attends workshops less often now as she has other priorities, but still likes being part of the Network.

Mary Porter was involved in the volunteering sector and then became a politician in the ACT with a strong community focus. SDN was attractive as a place of fellow travellers with a passion to change the world. It was scary attending the first workshop, but Mary found she could get to know others easily and share the experience of living, cooking and talking together. There was at times tension between the macro and the micro as different people gave them different priorities, but more recently the balance has been better. Ned remains central to SDN. "It has been a journey of growth, development, enlightenment, and pain, and letting go of old hurts while taking on new challenges, and nurturing people. He's a great nurturer".

Ray Rauscher, a town planner, saw Ned as an "oasis in uncharted territory". "To think there was a place for the big picture of society to be explored, and to gain tools to act, was exciting". He explains Ned's role in the following way: "Ned maintains an up-to-date understanding of world social and environmental needs. He gravitates to those organisations that work on the larger picture of needs and actions, as well as the micro needs of communities". Ray was impressed that SDN developed a manifesto well ahead of its time in terms of vision and inclusiveness.

Barbara Hicks, a social worker, attended her first workshop in the 1970s, at the time of the Whitlam Government's Australian Assistance Plan, which encouraged community development. Through the SDN, Ned provided a format to present case studies of community work, and this opened up ideas and possibilities. An important development was NED-Net which has enabled Ned to set up an ongoing means for funding projects. Barbara herself became a less frequent participant after her greater engagement with other priorities including a deep interest in anthroposophy. She values her continuing friendship with Ned and others in the network but is no longer an active contributor. "The issue for me is that there is no common spiritual or even philosophical base from which to launch shared initiatives or endeavours".

David Crew came to community development and SDN from an archaeological background, and is fully engaged in the Deniliquin scene, where he and his wife live. Sylvia Baker was an inspiration to him, and he accompanied her to his first workshops. Initially he was challenged to consider "what am I doing personally" and to reflect on his own individual skills and opportunities. He has been led to take further action locally as a result of using some of the group processes of SDN. He would value linking the content of workshops to community by better examples, scenarios and techniques.

Part I

Introductions

Chapter 1

The Social Developers' Network

Ned Iceton and Oral History

Jo Kijas

'*Our purpose in SDN is to be creative and action-oriented: we constantly seek explanations which emerge from action in the world. We are equally interested both in individual people and in the wider social and ecological systems on which our collective wellbeing depends*'[2]

In 1975 two long-standing friends, John Russell from Melbourne and Ned Iceton from Armidale, organized a workshop through personal contacts with those who were interested in social change. Out of the first Social Developers' Network (SDN) workshop new people became involved and Ned began a newsletter to link people between workshops. They began holding regional workshops and then held the first national workshop in 1980. They are still held each year in January[3]. The impetus for the first SDN workshop came out of Ned's earlier work with indigenous people centred in Armidale, and his evolving ideas about social change through both the personal and societal level. This book provides insight into Ned's theoretical development, embedded in a social history of a network of social developers now in their fourth decade of regular engagement.

---

2   Social Developers' Network homepage http://www.ned.org.au/sdn/sdn-blurb.htm#history
3   SDN home page.

Ned

Ned Iceton is always on the move. In his 78th year (2006), as this book was being developed, Ned's community involvement remained constant. Little had changed since admitting in his 2005 group Christmas letter that the idea of sorting things out at home for a potential move to a retirement home had little priority: 'I seem to be too addicted to my daily round of activity to make the time'.

In biographical notes prepared for his attendance at the Community Development Queensland Conference at Rockhampton in September 2007, Ned noted the following as his main activities for the year. In the local community of Armidale they included; 'involvements with the City Council's Safety Committee; the committee of the Armidale Community Foot Patrol; the Board of Jobs Australia Armidale; the Minimbah Aboriginal School; and with the offspring of a couple of Aboriginal folk with whom I worked intensively in the past'. His 'network involvements' included work with the 'movement for Restorative Justice/ Restorative Practices; with the International Simultaneous Policy Organisation; with the Action Learning, Action Research & Process Management Association; with political and other socially-involved folk; and in general Social Development networking and policy lobbying via email, on issues of our human future'.

The conference was Ned's second car trip to Queensland in a few months. As usual in July he had driven himself from Armidale to Townsville for the annual Australian Chamber Music Festival which he and his late wife Joan first patronised from the early 1990s. This annual journey always involved en route visits to old and new friends in his constant networking process. On his return from Townsville he prepared for a trip to Canberra to attend the mid-year meeting of the Board of the Nurturing Evolutionary Development Network (NED-Net).

NED-Net is a group of people who are working with Ned to help establish the practical and philosophical base of the N.E.D. Foundation, to which Ned will bequeath his Will. The guiding principles, quoted below, encapsulate the driving forces that underpin his ongoing determination to encourage individuals towards social development and change at all levels.

'The inspiration and direction of the N.E.D. Foundation is based on the following perceptions:

1. That the earth and the human species are facing a crisis, in which their survival as healthy living entities is now threatened as never before in recorded history.

2. That, in order to face this crisis, we all individually need to make use of our potential for inner growth. Only through the maturity gained by continual engagement in this, can we become effective – for the genuine, long-term benefit of ourselves and the world we live in.

3. That, above all other social theories and experiments, the principle of citizen involvement as expressed in the historic development of "Democracy" and "Co-operation", must be the primary impulse for our next evolutionary step. This principle needs to permeate and guide all areas of group and social activity – political, commercial and cultural. This principle expresses at human level, the larger principle which governs all life – that of ecology.

4. As an essential underpinning of these responses, we all need to attend retreats and workshops, as pragmatic personal experiences which allow us to regularly view our material goals and objectives from 'outside'. Such review needs to become a routine part of our personal, social and work life.'[4]

The contributors and oral history

The chapters which follow come from past and present members of SDN, as well as reflections from two people important in Ned's formative history prior to the establishment of SDN. The contributors were chosen through the NED-Net Board and volunteers who answered an email request. In part one 'Introductions' Ned reflects on the ideas which he sees as central to the ethos of SDN and his ongoing campaign to help people change the world. These concepts are embedded in his personal development and history. Part two 'Early connections' introduces two people, Terry Widders and John Ducker, who were key to Ned's developing strategies of social action through networking and workshops during the formative years of the 1960s.

4   NED-Net and N.E.D. Foundation guiding principles, http://www.ned.org.au/index.html

The substantive section of the book, part three 'Social Developers' Network', contains reflections from past and present members of SDN and offers a social history of evolving group work over more than thirty years. John Russell, cofounder of SDN, recounts the path which led him to Ned, and memories of the early style and evolution of the workshops from the early 1970s. Sylvia Baker used to take two days to travel by bus and train from her home in the Riverina to the Armidale workshops, but she took the time in her hectic life because it was so important to be re-energised amongst fellow community activists. Ben Leeman outlines his perceptions of the social developers' aims. The fourth chapter in this section comes from Tiyana Maksimovic-Binno who, unlike the others, no longer participates in SDN but found it important to reflect on a network that was highly significant to her. David Purnell and Chris Larkin reflect on the tensions created between the macro and micro agenda which participants brought, and the glue which kept the workshops together. Jean Leeman provides a perspective on the growth in confidence which many women developed through the workshops, and Mary Porter reflects on the ongoing revitalisation that the workshops still bring her after nearly two decades. The last chapter comes from past members, Ray Rauscher and Barbara Hicks, and a new member David Crew who, reflects on his first workshop attended in 2006. Together they provide insight into change and continuity from the first workshops to recent times.

All but two written contributions come from interviews which I conducted with the participants. Memory, accessed in this book predominantly through oral testimony, is a powerful tool in the construction of knowledge and history making. While people's memories and stories may sometimes be a poor source of accurate dates, names and numbers, they are powerful bearers of individual and community feeling. They help reveal that, as with all history, there is never just one true story. Therefore amongst the following pages one will read of both similar as well as differing perceptions and accounts of the same people and issues, and different observations of the same events.

The oral history interviews hold the raw source material from which I, as the editor, have made selective decisions about what to put in and leave out. Each of the interviewees' stories has been shaped into a narrative. This was achieved in at least two ways. Firstly, most interviews were originally between 10 000 and 15 000 words long, and I have edited them down to around 2-3000 words to form a narrative joining themes that were dispersed, returned to and circled around.

This has been a collaborative process with all contributors, where they have each had a role in final editing where they felt their stories needed greater or less emphasis on particular issues. Secondly, most of these reflective stories were well thought through before I ever came to speak to people. Oral stories, especially delivered through interviews, are rarely careless ramblings but more often thoroughly analysed and refined over time through thinking, reminiscing, talking, writing and debate.

Reflections which are presented on paper from oral history sources 'sound' different than deliberately written stories. Therefore, despite the editorial work, these stories should still sound like a spoken story where the speakers might be 'heard'. They can offer a more personal and intimate communication. It is hoped that these reflections will bring insight to others in their own path of social action.

Chapter 2

In Conversation

Ned Iceton

'A social developer is interested in everything in society. There isn't anything that isn't of potential interest.' *Ned Iceton.*

Ned fills each day with movement, therefore he has to make careful choices about how to use every waking hour. On that basis, he decided that the time-consuming task of organising and writing needed to produce a book was not for him. Rather, he decided that the best way to convey some of his thinking on ways forward, in community and social development, was to tell his story by answering the questions of others. That process began with two days of interviews with SDN member Jane Dunstan in February 2005, and a further two days with Jo Kijas in February 2007 covering different aspects of Ned's interests. This chapter therefore comes from a range of conversations between Ned and Jane (particularly on early influences and history) and between Ned and Jo. Ned then edited and expanded as he saw fit.

I.   The Social Developers' Network

Principles and process

Jo: *Would you outline the principles behind your understanding of what a social developer strives for.*

Ned: The Social Developers' *style* is that we are always supportive of everybody, but we are also quite confronting to each other about reality as we see it and about what we feel. The principles are mainly that when people are able to be honest with each other and trusting and supportive, irrespective of different points of view, real progress takes place. It produces a creativity, combined with a social cohesion, that makes developments possible that otherwise are not. People's fears are allayed when they understand things fully and have engaged with people in an honest exchange of emotional responses to whatever the situation is. When they can do that, they can learn from it. They can invent a solution; they can go ahead individually, and at the same time social cohesion is improved instead of weakened. When citizens don't understand and are left with fear, then they get cut off from each other and alienated, and then that's the road to social breakdown.

I've always been on about the necessity for personal development to go along with social development, especially for facilitators. For communities to be able to function at a higher level, *individuals* also have to be able to function themselves at a higher level. So these two things are cross-connected. You see, we've all been enculturated in a particular way, as children, but the world never stands still. There are always *new* issues, emphases and balance-points at any given time; and so *we need always to be making changes in the programming we were loaded up with from birth*. We need constant personal 'program updates' and we need help from *each other* to do that. We have to access both the emotional side and the cognitive side, and they must operate together. We don't generally operate them optimally as *individuals* – we do it better collectively.

No one else does what we do in the Social Developers. In other places you have 'talking heads' – supposedly experts – but they mostly come out of a cognitive-oriented background which so far refuses to look at emotional intelligence as important. You do have to develop the cognitive side equally, and we can do a lot of that on our own. But without action experience, and without personal relationships, you don't develop emotional intelligence. It's part of our hard wiring to be a social species. We do have the basic hardware and some of the software to give us these basic feelings, but mostly we don't learn to manage them very well. In past eras there was time for social evolution to occur in a gradual, unconscious way. But we're in an era where we haven't time to just let it happen by accident. *We need to be actively remaking ourselves in ways we need to be*, in order to have a human future – that's the guts of social development. It's about re-writing our individual and societal culture, as a prescription for our species' ills.

The fact is that global reality has changed radically. It has come to affect all aspects, including voluntary citizen groups. Globalisation expands competitive boundaries beyond previous geographical borders. This is especially so for private organisations. Also the contemporary contraction of government agencies and the focus on 'partnerships' challenge established public sector roles and ways of working. Self Help and community groups are increasingly 'doing it for themselves', pushing uphill from an historically under-funded base and largely ignored by formal decision makers. Instead, innovation needs to be nurtured in every sector, while still meeting the challenges of accountability. Survival means having to be fleet-of-foot and big systems oriented. Thriving means adopting new ways of looking at strategies, leadership, competence, effectiveness and working together as groups in a sector. Complexity theory, chaos theory and human systems dynamics give us new metaphors by which to explore how best we can develop new tools and remain flexible, adaptable and congruent with reality.

I think that we probably can't stop 'the big crash' that is coming relatively soon. Centralised hierarchical systems will probably largely fail and will have to be rebuilt on new lines. And then we'll need social regeneration points. Thus social developers will be the germ of those social regeneration points. Each local situation will evolve for citizens in different, unpredicted ways; and the key will be to work out what response best fits, constantly remaking ourselves and our culture, in light of the values we share, and the emotional payoffs in self-meaning that we give each other. And, for that to happen, we need to have social support mechanisms of honesty and genuineness in place.

The workshops

The Social Development Practitioners' workshops, as I called them initially, were my way of building up a group of people who would be motivated, and would comprehend why this work was socially important. The SD workshops were geared, back in 1975, to support the Australian Assistance Plan – an initiative of the Whitlam government – which was setting up Regional Councils for Social Development across the country. Within each SD workshop group we would provide ourselves with the kind of supportive but honest feedback to help us define reality, and build our skills and our theory of practice. I needed it for me as much as others. In a couple of years, as numbers built up, we became the Social Developers' Network (SDN).

The first workshop was in 1975 – probably in March in the vacant nurses' home of a psychiatric hospital in Newcastle area. As mentioned, I regard SDN as a kind of 'ideal family' which I created for myself. In other words, I needed a group of people to reassure me that I wasn't mad to be interested and committed to community and society in the ways that I was. The mainstream, in lots of ways, didn't 'get it'. So the first group of people I invited simply took a risk on 'what Ned is wanting to do' and agreed to try it out. Thus we tested the idea for eight days, living in together, which is not something that happens every day!

John Russell had met me several years before at a sociology conference. After the first SDN workshop, he was insistent that I run more of them. It's quite possible that without him pushing me I may not have recognized that we had hit on something significant – an important and culturally new style and process.

What's the difference between social developers and community developers?

I ended up calling us *social* developers because mostly in the workshops we are helping individual citizens to define and tackle a social problem situation – or see a need for some developmental thing that they become aware of – which will involve mobilizing a group of enthusiast citizens to do something about it. Generally speaking that group will be only a *subset* of what could be thought of as (whole) community. Community is the population of a local area. Rarely do you get whole community development occurring, because generally it happens in sectors, around serially emerging issues.

Those who come to the SD's workshops are individuals from a variety of areas. They come into the workshops and then go back to do their thing, but mostly it won't be the whole community they'll end up mobilising. So *community development* seems like a rather overblown phrase. The SDN just provides personal mentoring to self-motivated people for their citizen role. As Tony Windsor, our local Independent federal member says, 'Those who run the world are those who turn up'.

The content of the workshops emerges from some current issue for a person – not always a crisis – and that's the stimulus to fostering some sort of action to deal with it. In extreme circumstances it's converting an emergency into an emergence. There are waves of malfunctioning that overtake different sectors of the community at different times. When it manifests in a sector we have the chance to intervene and make a difference in outcome.

So in a Social Developers workshop you come as an individual, and you can come and talk about whatever issue is important to you, is that right?

Yes, that's right. And it's also okay for them to say, 'I'll just start talking and see where I get to – because I don't necessarily know what is going to come out!' You can do that in a Social Developers workshop. Participants don't have to know clearly in advance where they're at, exactly. They may feel something isn't right but are uncertain what it is, exactly. They can just start talking around whatever seems to be a concern for them, with all of us listening, and they'll move through to crystallise whatever it is. And then we'll help them through defining it. It's also about developing their emotional intelligence as the primary skill and resource in being a community or social developer. And the action plan that emerges will be built around their strengths rather than their weaknesses, which are unique to every person.

An important feature, always, in the SD workshops is diversity of participants. There is always a diversity of people and it's about getting the inclusive climate right – the *vibes*. The thing is that diversity is a defining feature of any community: we're all different. Each workshop presents participants with the challenge of engaging with a range of quite different people, all of whom are citizens.

I've been the principal networker in the whole thing, so the people who come are often ones that I've recruited. That is, they are people who are different, yet whose differences I can cope with. But also across these differences they can all see something in what I'm on about, which is the unifying thing amongst all of us. So you have to have those two features – everyone must be able to see the unifying thing, as well as the reality that they each have their own very real individuality and personhood. So we aren't just a lot of yes-men or -women. The core thing with me is that *real communities always depend on diverse people* – and it's that diversity that alone provides the competencies that community and society can collectively deliver[5].

---

5   See Jane's interview/story about the Farmers Group on the SDN website.

Culture and the individual

I came to think in a way that I'm a 'cultural therapist' and that the SD workshops are about helping people rewrite their culture so that it fits the reality they've got to deal with – i.e., that it's not about the individual personality but the whole cultural system, and the two are interconnected. You can't grow up in a society without bearing the marks of that society, as well as the marks of your particular family of origin. And there's nothing to be gained by seeing this culture as right or wrong, in any absolute sense. But you can always be clear on whether the culture is liable to work or not work in the circumstances prevailing *now*. The purpose of the SD workshops hasn't changed. It was always about helping people tackle an issue of any kind that mattered to them, and, *as part of that interactive process, to rewrite our culture* in various ways to enable us to best relate and operate together. *And that means leaving behind some traditional things in the culture and devising and taking on some new, necessary and positive things.*

It was also clear to me at some level that an awareness of what is humanising, or the reverse, is available to me *in my body*. I can always feel whether something is right or not right. There is a guidance system in the body – at some level –to work out: 'is this a humanising direction or is it not?' And in a Social Developers group, which is both mutually supportive and confronting, people feel more secure and so have better access to their inner awareness of what is and isn't right than they would in a situation of panic, fear, or isolation, in which more maladaptive responses tend to come out.

How do you keep people from becoming overwhelmed as individuals, in complex cultural settings?

People need supportive relationships, which is what the workshops offer. So in the workshops we can say: 'Is this thing that you're hankering to do worth doing? Let's go through the risks and fears you have. Which of them are real and which aren't? And, within the limitations that you feel, what is it that you *would risk* doing? Is it a risk that you're willing to take? If so you can start planning action which involves a risk within your comfortable limit.' If they do that first, they may later be ready to take more of a risk – and sometimes there will be a risk that's *not* worth taking. This is 'sorting out' what the workshops actually do, but it's often far less explicit than this.

And in all that, the global and the local have to fit together. There is a oneness that unites all social and ecological reality– so that everything affects everything else. Whichever 'end' or entry point we *can* work on is the place to begin. That would be a Social Developers strategy. Wherever the opportunity is to foster something socially developmental – that's where you work. For example, if it's possible to work on a political 'macro' level, OK – but if you have an authoritarian government that isn't in crisis – then you have to work at the local 'micro' level, preparing for the future in various ways, there, and waiting for a 'macro' shift that will come later.

As I've said, I feel that the need is for each of us to be learning both at a personal level and at the level of what we're trying to do in society: that's a core Social Developer idea. You can't be an optimal part of social development unless you're working on yourself. Our own *subliminal* programming is always out of date, just as society's habits are. This requires facing the pain and difficulty of change; but, what else are we to do? What else is worth doing? We've got a life – what's the meaning of life? The meaning of life is being alive and then making our own meaning from what we do with it.

II. Life: Getting on with it

Formative influences

In February 2005, Jane Dunstan spent 2 days with Ned. She asked him what his formative influences had been.

I think social developers – conscious of their role or not – will be social regeneration points when the big crash comes. Just as my Mum was in the Depression in the 1930s. She was a regeneration point for getting the Gunnedah community together and saying, 'We're going to cope with all this'. Mum was my first model of a community developer. She organised events for the whole town. Right through the Depression and then the war, she would devise morale-boosting events such as theatrical drama and concerts. In the early thirties when I was a baby, she used to cook Sunday dinner and take it up to people living in humpies on Pensioners Hill. They were just ordinary people with no work and desperately affected by the Depression.

My Mum was spontaneous, and outgoing. It was a charismatic style. Dad didn't have that, and I don't have it, whereas my brother did. Dad didn't have an emotional interest in other people either, whereas Mum did, and so do I. She maintained relationships widely with other people. She'd bridge divisions across the town, and that role is important for a community developer. My side has been my networking, with a diaspora spread all over Australia and beyond. But my approach is similar to hers in the sense she would always want something real – something emotionally significant – in each relationship, as do I.

So I was born in Gunnedah in 1930, at the start of the Great Depression. My father was a lawyer and was often paid only in kind – in wheat, or day-old chicks, or honey or whatever. So it was a very difficult time. I had a younger brother, Venn. He was four years younger, and he was my best friend – there was never any rivalry between us.

As a young doctor I went to England between 1956 and 1958, and I did a postgraduate training course in child health. Just at the end of that course, Venn, who had just done his final year exams in Medicine in Sydney, was killed on his motorbike. I had always been going to set up a practice with him. And because he was my best friend, I had quite a major reaction to his death – at a time when I was on my own, in Britain. My impulse at the time really was just to go home, but my family said to carry on – to stay and finish.

My Dad was very keen that I become a conventional GP. But I failed that exam in child health, and I failed it again later when they urged me to stay in the UK and do it again. It was a fairly depressing time for me, in England, in the winter smog. and I was doing a lot of soul-searching after Venn died. That was where all the thinking was done about changing my career direction.

At the time many other overseas people were doing the same exam – Indians, Sri Lankans, Africans – and they had been asking me: 'What's the story with Aboriginal people in Australia?' And I really didn't know! So eventually from the UK I arranged to take a job in the Northern Territory, employed by the NT Medical Service, which was run from Canberra.

I was there between 1958 and 1962. I went first to Darwin, and then I was sent to Alice Springs. We had daily radio hook-ups with the outback stations and settlements via the Royal Flying Doctor Service, and we began travelling out to do routine clinics. But we found we were viewed as transients – the outback folk were very cynical about the people who came up from the city. 'Oh yes, and when are you leaving?' they'd ask, when we were first introduced. It took about two years for some station people to trust us enough to let us visit. I told them I wasn't planning to leave.

I began spontaneously to be a social developer through that daily radio contact. Whereas we were just normally talking about who was sick and what to do about that, I began to talk also about other things. For example I'd say: 'there's a survey being undertaken on the state of education services for the outback people, so it would be good if you put your heads together and made a submission.' The radio offered a potential forum for airing local social issues that arose, and it seemed like common sense to me to use it. This was probably 1960-61.

I also had the experience, when working in Alice Springs, of seeing the various patterns of Aboriginal illness – the cycles through the generations – which were a direct outcome of their lifestyle. With that lifestyle, I saw that they'd always suffer that same pattern of illness. And this precipitated my awareness of a parallel process occurring in white culture. I saw how our contemporary mainstream culture could be seen as an out-of-date 'prescription' for our social reality, and that's why we were all getting sick. The community development stuff, for me, later became the idea of 'social therapy' and the 'prescription' was to facilitate a participatory, conscious management of our cultural evolution. That is, *the idea that we should be consciously designing and redesigning our culture as an evolving collective prescription for dealing with our ever-changing social reality.*

Before long I got transferred back to Darwin against my will. For some time I was sent to do surveys of Aboriginal health on a series of top end missions, but I didn't have the training I felt I needed for tropical diseases like leprosy, hookworm, etc. Then I was grounded in Darwin, and had nothing significant to do. I was under a lot of stress and decided to do the Sydney University Diploma of Tropical Medicine and Hygiene. For me to do this I had to resign.

That university course was a very good experience, during which the professor of Tropical Medicine referred me to various books about community development. So right after that, through 1963-64, I went travelling across India, Pakistan and Sri Lanka. I went *then* because I felt that I probably would not be able to do it later if I were I to be married. I wanted to see how community development was being applied to achieve better health in those countries. I had referrals to United Nations people working in each country helping local nationals with their health promotion programs. I wasn't *practicing* medicine on that circuit. I was simply going around with doctors and sociologists and local staff to see how they were tackling things. I didn't get paid; it was purely my own study interest. I found I could live very cheaply there. I used to be able to have a local style breakfast for about five cents, and I could have a full meal – a 'rice plate' – for about 20 cents. I had saved enough money in Oz to be able just to dribble it out and continue moving from place to place over there, for two years.

I was interested at first in community development as a means of achieving changes in *health* practices; and then it gradually dawned that people actually have their own priorities, *different* from mine! So the community developer's job is to help people address those, and often they've got many other priorities *ahead* of health. So the job is to help them move sequentially through what their aspirations are. I was becoming much more committed to the need for problem-definition and solving *by local communities*, and how to effectively empower people for that.

In May 1966 I got a job in community development (CD) in Armidale, at the University of New England, as 'Lecturer (Community Development)'. When I came first to that CD job my big disappointment was that absolutely nobody there really knew what I was on about. And not only that, they weren't interested! I had sort of hoped that – 'Here's my big chance to be intellectual about the social processes I'm interested in'. But, you know, there was nobody at the university. In fact my main discussant became this young local Aboriginal chap, Terry Widders, who was very bright, and is now a lecturer at Macquarie University. He was about 19 at the time – late 1966.

The Aboriginal Human Relations workshops and the Bannockburn farmers

Two key activities in Ned's early life at the UNE contributed to the later development of the SDN workshops format. These were his work with Aboriginal people and his relationship with a group of Inverell farmers.

One of my first jobs as lecturer in community development included establishing relationships with Aboriginal people. I was to work with the Armidale Association for Aborigines, a local white group, who actually had had a committee to meet me and vet me before I got appointed. It was 1966 when that relationship began. In the early days at UNE I had attended Human Relations workshops, using the current 'T-Group' format, that were run by a psychologist lecturer, and I decided that this was the kind of thing I'd need to offer Aboriginal men. The reason was this: my experience in those first four years with

Aboriginal people in Armidale convinced me that the women were more intact as persons than the men. It seemed as though the men had had their political/cultural role and their social/ breadwinner role destroyed by white occupation, but the women's role as child bearers and carers had continued and they were less destroyed as persons. When we set out to build up some Aboriginal community organisations, which was part of my job as a community developer, I could mobilise quite a few *women* – but there were never any men.

By 1970 I decided that we needed to get the men together on their own and free them up to be able to participate in something developmental for them. So in 1970 I ran the first Aboriginal Human Relations Workshop, and I had Terry Widders come along – someone I'd known from about the age 18[6]. There were only eight of us at the first one and it was a very intense and powerful experience for all of us. We talked about the problem things that upset people, and what action they might be able to take to remedy them. And then we rehearsed what we needed to do. Perhaps we'd need to ask the City Council Clerk about helping the local Aboriginal folk in some way; and then we would talk through what had to be said and who was going to say it. We would rehearse it and then the delegate would go and do it, backed up by a couple of others. It was a pretty powerful experience. At the end of it one of the participants, Ray Kelly, said: 'This experience has lit a light in me that will never go out'.

After that first one I ran these workshops for men and women together. In them we discussed the problems Aboriginal people faced – and thus began the Social Developers idea, but not yet crystallized as such. We were still using the workshop format called *T-Group*, which was quite confrontational. I subsequently decided that that particular style wasn't ideally productive. It *was* very productive for some people, but scared the daylights out of some others, so it wasn't always helpful. But, anyway, I was stopped by the University from running any more for Aboriginal folk after 1974 – I presume because they were getting uppity! They had started to ask for things, and that wasn't what the authorities were used to – the University didn't want any more of that! Then in 1975 I started the Social Developers workshops, which grew out of the Aboriginal workshops, but also grew out of my experience with farmers at Inverell.

Soon after I first came here to Armidale I stimulated the launch of a farmers' group out of Inverell, to help them deal with soil erosion and

6   See chapter three, Terry Widders chapter.

low productivity [The Bannockburn Farmers][7]. I gradually got them into looking at fresh ways to achieve their goals. By bringing them together in a group for the first time, I helped them develop a family-style spirit. That new spirit of mutuality in their farming group was what motivated and kept them going. This was because they began relating honestly with each other, and sharing their strengths and weaknesses. Members of the group had different skills, e.g., welding, say, while others were good with the soil, or with livestock. The people who were good at particular things became resources to someone else. They all were good at *something*, so they all became resources to each other. All the wives got into doing the books, and came to know what the farm could afford and what it couldn't afford, and domestic conflicts over money basically disappeared. Relationships improved with their children too. And these changes overall enabled them to turn from being the least competent 'payers' in town, to the best. I had about five years of full-on involvement with this group, and it was a marvellous learning experience.

Joan: a wife on the same wavelength

Ned met his wife Joan in the late 1960s. By then she was a lecturer in Education at the CAE having previously been a primary school teacher. They were both involved in Aboriginal support issues and were in the Armidale Association for Aborigines, as well as attending the same human relations workshop sessions run by the UNE Counsellor over a year.

In the course of those things we came to know each other better. Then one day Ray Kelly, my Aboriginal friend, said I should ask Joan out; 'She'd be right for you'. So we hooked up, and we were married in 1972. Ray was our best man. Joan and I had our own interests that substantially overlapped. In 1973 we went overseas on our sabbatical-honeymoon, and along the way we had one of those strange crossovers. When we got to Los Angeles there was one chap that I wanted to look up and a woman that she wanted to look up. When we found them, finally, living in a beach suburb of Los Angles, they were married – and we hadn't even known that they knew each other!

7   See chapter 4, John Ducker's chapter. For an extended reminiscence of Ned's time with the Bannockburn farmers, see Jane Dunstan's interview 'The Bannockburn Farmer's: Interview with Ned Iceton', SDN Stories, http://www.ned.org.au/sdn/sdnstories/bannockburn.htm

Joan was always involved in the Social Developers from the time she met me. She always had expectations of the SD members that were more demanding than mine were, and she'd also get worried about me and my errors – I had much of my 'control freak' stuff in me then. She'd be watching me and stopping me from overdoing it – and probably quite appropriately. She was always there. But the SDN was my thing rather than hers. That would be a realistic thing to say.

Joan was very keen to do this particular Master's program in 'Confluent Education' in Santa Barbara, California, so we went off there in about 1975. I went as a sort of house husband. *Confluent* meant having emotion and cognition flowing together, so we were on a wavelength there. Then when she came back to the CAE, there was a new principal who didn't approve of anything 'humanistic.' Gradually she was harassed in various ways until she was squeezed out.

But because we knew this was liable to happen to either one of us, we already had a mutual agreement that whoever got squeezed out first, the other would hang in there and maintain a salary for both. I had to hang in over a fairly extended period of, basically, harassment in the department I was in. Because when the original Director who appointed me had gone, there was an interim phase before another man was appointed by the University with basically the unstated job of closing down the department over time. The department was probably called by then *Continuing Education*. It had been called originally *Adult Education*, then *University Extension,* and then *Continuing Education*, until it was finally closed down.

I was asked finally to run events that would raise my own salary – not any part of the original contract! It all became untenable, and finally I got redundancy in Sep '92. And in that month Joan got the news that the cancer from her second mastectomy had spread. I was preoccupied with that, and any steps I might have taken to maintain connections with the University, I did not. Joan died June of '93. And after that I was fairly flat, becoming quite depressed in late '93.

I then realised that I needed to give myself permission to do a few things I simply enjoyed, rather than just things that were worthy! I took a couple of holiday trips away and met some new friends on my travels. It was the task of organising myself to put on the next annual Social Developers' workshop in January '94 that got me out of it, finally.

Our life together had been good. We'd started taking trips to Townsville for the Australian Festival of Chamber Music. We both liked music, liked our travel, here and abroad, and we entertained a lot of overseas people. We were both interested and involved in the local Australia/China friendship association. We enjoyed landscape together – we enjoyed the company of many of the same people – and we both enjoyed cooking which we did together when entertaining. Very satisfactory, you'd have to say – which meant Joan's death was a major loss. But at least I knew, after Joan died, that because I'd been a bachelor for a long time before, I *could* hang in and manage as a widower. At first I thought I'd get married again soon, but then thought 'No!' – I needed to be properly free of Joan before I could consider marrying anyone else. In the end I decided I wouldn't remarry at all.

But then later there was a very good friend of Joan's, interested in travel and music and the same sorts of things – who'd been part of the cancer support group we had had meeting here at our place. Marie had had melanoma. She now came to be in very good health for a couple of years, and from '96 we did a lot of good trips all over. But in '98 she got secondary melanomas in the brain, and died. We'd had a couple of good years and I think Joan would have been happy that we did.

Marie and I both had our own things, and we decided not to live together. I was starting to think about this Nurturing Evolutionary Development[8] organisation that I was going to leave my estate to, and she had her own family things, and so we just met once a week and went away at intervals on these holiday trips together.

After Marie's death I continued with my ongoing activities. Which doesn't mean that there isn't a regular emotional pay off from them that I need – i.e. when I get a high. It's useful, for example, when I get emotionally recharged at the end of a workshop – one which despite all the crises has succeeded. There's a satisfaction in it. There's confirmation in it. This is what life is.

Whatever meaning there is in life – this is it! To be who we are, to the fullest extent we can, in the most cooperative arrangements with

8   The Nurturing Evolutionary Development Association, Inc. was incorporated in the ACT in 2007. Its eight members are longstanding recurrent participants in the Social Developers' workshops. I have invited them to take on the task of continuing to run social developers' workshops after my death, funded by my estate. Its wider scope is to support socially developmental processes in society, via seed funds that could enable citizen groups to launch themselves. These funds are to support volunteer citizen activity, not to pay salaries for service delivery.

whoever else we are thrown into the world with. Collectively we can do more than we can do on our own, and that's very enjoyable. But we each also have to do our own individual thing.

What Ned is 'on about"

Over the years of working with people I came to understand that the job of social developers is to work on ourselves as much as on other people, because we all really need to transcend the (obsolete) programming we were loaded up with as kids. I used to offer an exercise I called a 'life script analysis' – I haven't done it for a while – it comes out of transactional analysis. And it explains to any person who wants to know, how they came to be the person they are, with all the strengths and weaknesses they have – especially on the emotional side. It explains how a program was loaded into them unconsciously – from those very early years, and, good or bad, it's nobody's fault. It happened. And there's no point in being defensive about it. It's just a fact. Then you have to work out which bits of your unconscious programming are useful and OK, and which bits need to be rewritten – i.e. a 'program upgrade'.

In relation to my meditation, I talk about 'who Ned really really *really* is'; a higher level entity from 'little Ned' who has had these programs unconsciously installed in him. At that meta-level of who Ned really is, the programs in 'little Ned' are somehow left behind and there's an entity which can respond to reality now, seeing beyond these old programs. And that's what I'm relying on. That's where my guidance comes from.

My unrecognised flaw was that I wanted to control and fix things – and there is a line between *appropriate* fostering of participatory responses and a *compulsive need to push people* in the direction that society may well need to go – but which isn't the way to do it. This secret flaw used to undermine me in the early days; but I've worked hard on that, and there is less compulsion in me now than there was.

I was never authoritarian 'Left' in my conscious orientation, just as I was never authoritarian 'Right'. But at an unconscious level, I *was* authoritarian in trying to do the developmental thing, and to push it along, instead of having the patient recognition that people have to do things in their own time, when they are ready, out of their own motivation – out of their own understanding. They have to be their own authentic actors in their own right, despite the anxiety on my behalf to get a result!

So I've come to recognise that we each have to learn how to manage ourselves. How to recognise these unconscious programs, despite them being deeply unconscious – a lot of emotionally driven motivations. Indeed, most people in the world invent intellectual *pretexts, after the event,* for what they've already emotionally committed to 'out of conviction'. And they've never actually got to the bottom of where that programmed conviction is coming from.

There's no other contemporary social arena in which you're allowed to be as real and as 'whole person' as you are in the SD workshops. And there's something addictive about being allowed to be who you actually are, at the point you're at. *Because that's the only point you can grow from.* That's the only positive kind of addiction there is, and that addiction is *to be something more than I have been up to now.* It's very exciting. And the energy comes from there. So this spirituality is the 'Holy Ghost', in secular terms. It is thus negentropy – love, which is the life energy in the universe. The other energy – entropy – is fear, and is the clockwork-running-down-energy in the universe. And we humans have both of those there, as realities of experience, and as options.

I'm also essentially contesting the belief that any existing culture is suitable for the future. *I'm saying they're all out of date* – every one of them. They're all prescriptions for a reality that is not the reality now. We humans have to invent our own new prescription. That's the job of social development. The job is collectively to invent the culture we need NOW – that means the values and the wisdom by which we must operate, how we treat each other, what we think is important, what we will take action on, or what we don't give so much importance to, and what gives us a buzz of self-meaning– all of which is cultural.

Society is always evolving. Certain things were possible in the Depression when my Mum was working as a community developer – things which are impossible to do now, because there's been a wholesale cultural deterioration. But human beings are still there – and always have that core ability – to recognise what behavioural values are socially constructive, and which are not,– and can always tell which *if they are keeping in touch with themselves.* Which comes back to our need for self-development and self-honesty, along with group relationships of honesty. Thus, in the SDN, we help, support and trust one another as a collective in a developmental way that we can't do fully on our own.

Into the future from the past and present

My object has always been to plug every new understanding into every pre-existing one. So I'm looking always to developing my understanding as a matrix and not as a straight line – everything plugged into everything else. There aren't any ends that are not tied to something else, and that's the opposite of an academic approach where it's essentially linear. And what I always say is that we'll only have a future if we deal adequately with the present. So, if we're dealing in the best possible way with the present, that's the best we can be doing. There's such complexity in the world – the options are infinite and we can never know more than the general outline – we can't know into the future. But we can plan to be ready in wisdom to deal with what is to come, knowing that the unexpected is what to be ready for.

One of my main desires at the moment is helping to form an Australian level of the Restorative Justice/Practices (RJ) movement. This began as an alternative method for engaging with juvenile delinquents, requiring them to engage face-to-face with the folk hurt by their behaviour, and then to move into some kind of agreed restitution and then into reconciliation. When as a result recidivism fell dramatically, it became clear that this was a far more productive approach than the normal courts were. It helps people learn how to be more emotionally intelligent in their relationships.

The Restorative Justice method was an advance on what I was doing before – even though in fact I was already actually doing it. It offered a way to achieve emotional learning by being cognitively explicit. I see it as usefully pointing to the unrecognised and unacknowledged emotional barriers to change within individuals and societies; barriers that often stop community development occurring. It's the same underlying stuff as the social developers help with, so it's completely compatible.

You see, a pussyfooting interpersonal style is ultimately what causes blow-ups and social breakdown – because no one is saying what they really mean to each other. But in truth real growth and progress require that we routinely and honestly share our reality. And this is the socially developmental paradigm shift that I see can be assisted by Restorative Justice – i.e. calling a spade a spade, and being honest always about what really matters to us – what is our main emotional concern. And *you have to practice doing it in order to learn it* – emotional intelligence is something you have to learn – it's not a genetic given. And I want to accelerate its application in schools – a current project of mine. Starting in schools is starting where we have to start –having them experience a new cultural paradigm beginning early in their life.

So the importance to me of RJ is that it is a developmental value-process, potentially on a broad scale, that can help turn us around from consumerism, negativism and fear and all the things that are causing us to destroy the globe and our future on it.

I believe that these principles of RJ and within the Social Developers are applicable anywhere, and that our task is to recognise and act to apply them wherever openings arise. The whole process of SD involves recognising that different sectors of society come into crisis at different times and then need change. When that happens – that is, in a Chinese way of seeing it– there is an *emergency* of some kind that provides an opportunity for *emergence*. There's always a growth opportunity inherent in a crisis. Or, of course, one *could* go further down into disaster. Both possibilities always exist when a crisis arises.

And in the normal course of events none of us understands enough to know everything about everything, and so we've got Buckley's chance of knowing where the wave of change will break. But wherever it breaks, that's where we need to be, because we want the change that's coming out of it to be positive instead of the reverse, in each case. So, I suppose, at the back of my mind I've felt there's the need of a cohort of people who are ready to go and facilitate a constructively developmental response wherever there is a crisis, and the need for change is recognised. As social developers, these are the people whose personal development we are helping to facilitate.

A high point in my life for me, always, is a Social Developers workshop. Because we demonstrate every time that the *process* works. And we end up creating a supportive, constructive environment where everyone gets a go. That's where my faith comes in – that if we follow this process then we won't go astray, and we won't get co-opted back into an obsolete mainstream. The process ensures that everyone has space, is respected, and is confronted with reality as it is. The two things go together – that everyone must be confronted with the honest responses of others, but in a context of respect and appreciation that we are all who we are, at the point we're at, and that that's okay. There's no other place we can be.

Part Two

Early Connections

Chapter 3

Parallel worlds to connectivity

Terry Widders

Terry was a young Aboriginal man finding his way between the two worlds of rural northern NSW and radicalising Sydney when he met Ned early in his time at UNE. Ned explains: 'My luck in running across Terry was that he had a sociological imagination to the degree that I required in somebody who could be a 'sounding board', and could help me think through where I wanted to go and how to get there. He, also, was himself thinking through issues. The fact is that Terry's support role to me was enormously important in helping me develop my understanding over a number of years'

Terry

I want to tell you what I think are the relevant points in my life leading up to Ned, with the idea that Ned didn't just stand for a person, but a set of ideas and thoughts, as he expressed them, which it's possible to connect with.

Setting the scene: Terry's background

I grew up in the Armidale area. From about nine we rented a house in town – not on 'the Reserve', because most of those families living there were from the New England area. My relatives were from the Mid North Coast and from the West. But our family had been in Armidale for at least two generations before me. It was all to do with the changing pastoral landscape.

I went to high school in Armidale because I got a state bursary. There was one other Aboriginal lad, a cousin of mine. And we had further assistance from the AAAA – the Armidale Association for the Assimilation of Aborigines[9]. That enabled me and my cousin to go to St John's Hostel, and we attended one of the public high schools. So we were from the local area but 99% of the others at the hostel came from the pastoral families of the north-western areas of New South Wales. Most of those who I was studying with at school were going to go to university.

But I couldn't see how I was going to fit. Just about everyone else I knew from my family group left school either at or before they turned 14 years and 10 months. And there was high employment in the rural industries at that time – that's the late 50s. I wasn't squattocracy and I didn't come from a professional background, so I couldn't see what the continuity would be all about. It didn't fit – so I just stopped.

I finished high school in 1964. I went back and forth to Sydney and met other Aboriginal people who were leaders like Stockely Carmichael and the Black Power Movement. I met people like Gary Foley, Gary Williams, Chicka Dixon and so on – this whole network of Aboriginal people right up the eastern seaboard from Melbourne to Brisbane. And there was the build up to the 67 Referendum – wow, listening to people like Faith Bandler. So there was now a whole other connection I had – absolutely and totally new. It was a whole re-talking of being in the world.

I came back and forth to Armidale to help my grandmother. I got several local jobs and I also went working with my cousins in the shearing sheds and construction sites which allowed me a wide network of people way out into the North West.

So there were all these different ways of talking about the world that I found altogether fascinating. But they were parallel worlds, and the specificity of what they were all talking about wasn't the same as that being discussed within my family network. If you ain't got no one to talk to, you'll either turn into a fruit loop, or stay quite happy within your little cluster. But circumstances for most people in life require that they have a connection going out, as well as going in.

---

9   The Association changed its name in 1965 to the Armidale Association for Aborigines (AAA).

My difficulty was who would I find to talk to about all this? And this led to my connection with Ned Iceton.

Meeting Ned

In '66 I was staying with my grandmother, who was on the Reserve by that time. She was looking after some of her grandchildren and they were living right next door to Shoonkly [Ray] Kelly[10]. And a week or two before that I'd heard about Ned Iceton from a cousin of mine by marriage to the Smiths', Auntie Nell. And she'd been out visiting my grandmother: 'yes Auntie, I've met this man – he was with the Flying Doctor Service – he's a really tall person, etc.'

Then no more than a few weeks later Ned Iceton turns up at a house opposite – Ethel McKenzie's place – Ray's wife's mother. She used to talk a lot – make noises – be 'the front'. I was going into town and I was walking along when he pulled up and said 'Can I give you a lift?' I said – 'Yes, sure, thank you, and who are you?' You don't often have people pulling up at that end of town who aren't Aboriginal people and asking if you want a lift. So he introduced himself – but I was more interested that he'd been over talking to Ethel McKenzie and I told him so.

I said something like, 'You know, you really should be careful talking to that woman 'cause she sprouts a bit of bullshit now and again.' I guess I was only saying what was a common opinion or impression amongst our family group – a characterisation. Anyway, he didn't take umbrage but he did say, 'Well I think she's as much right to have her voice heard as anyone else.'

So he kind of challenged me on that, and I suppose that brought to the surface the slightly unconscious order of things that I'd developed in my head, about where people fitted in and what they should and shouldn't do.

So Ned was connected to the AAA [Association for the Assimilation of Aborigines]. I didn't quite know what his role was with them. But

---

10   Ray Kelly became a life-long friend of Ned's. See Ned's interview about Ray and his work with the National Parks and Wildlife Service in 'Lighting a Light: Reflections from Ned Iceton' in Johanna Kijas, *Revival, Renewal and Return: Ray Kelly and the NSW Sites of Significance Survey*, (Hurstville: DEC) 2005.

what the convergence role, then, was that I wanted to do something about the '67 Referendum, and the people who were organising the booths for the '67 Referendum in Armidale where the AAA was active.

It was alright to cooperate with them – but certainly not with the Welfare Board! That was another thing that was on the boil, but wasn't so public –the coming to the end of the Welfare Board. We knew the Welfare Board officer – his role was to monitor people – reporting if people were going in and out of town at night and so on. But my mob in Sydney had also given me a better understanding about what all that had been about, and how they were the bad successors to the Aborigines Protection Board.

Now somewhere in there – Ned's connection with the AAA thing, and the community development thing, was that he wanted to meet and talk very specifically with people – to have an anchor in what we can call, very broadly, the community. We know there are multiple communities – different families, different networks and responsibilities – and this was all just normal. So Ned was trying to find one of these connectors, and he found Jim Smith. And Jim was one of us. He was the son of my Aunt Nell, and what he said counted. And Jim Smith talked consistently with Ned Iceton. So, that put Ned on the map.

Parallel worlds and connecting to community

For me in particular, I had a number of years living parallel lives – in the hostel, shearing with my cousins, with my Sydney gang, and reading the Black Panthers. But it also allowed me to observe and think about this social world that Ned Iceton wanted to talk about – community development, relations between people, and what we might call cultural change and adaptation. There were other words which the Welfare Board was using such as maladaptive, [unable to fit in with contemporary society], all sounding like putdowns on one hand, but true in the sense that there were people who weren't adapting, partly because they didn't want to. And I shared something of that because, well, why would you want to step outside this world? Like – 'you should go on to university' – but why would I want to do that? What's there?

So these all rang little bells – but I also thought they were negative, especially with my new understanding of things from my Sydney
friends – the idea from the Black Panthers that it was all part of a constructed power relationship. So I wasn't having any of that!

But Ned Iceton, nevertheless, wanted to talk about the 'real world'
experience of those social relationships, and I thought that was a good
thing to do. And some of my relatives like Jim Smith thought that was
a good thing to do too. So it got a tick – kosher.

What Ned was talking about, though, around '68 was something
which also wasn't on the public agenda. But it was absolutely self-evi-
dent, experientially – issues of how [our] people lived and conducted
their everyday social relationships with each other. Of course we knew
this – we characterised them [amongst the diverse Aboriginal commu-
nity] – all the different types of people. We knew some people would be
looking after too many children on behalf of others; yes we knew that
sometimes there wasn't enough money or food. There was an unfair-
ness in the distribution of the rights and responsibilities and obliga-
tions at this social level. But, when you stopped and thought about it
you realised – there is something else in the broader social structure of
these relationships which is uneven and unfair. We knew that – very
well – thank you, and you could find it everywhere you went. So that
was the agenda he was addressing. And that was different, but just as
important, as the '67 Referendum, the Welfare Board, Black Panthers,
and all of those agendas.

Ned's talking post

When I was back in Armidale in '68 I got a job in the local PMG
store driving a crane. That's when Ned consistently, or persistently,
used to come and talk with people. And I was one of them. I was probably about 18 or 19. And he particularly wanted me to write down my
thoughts. I was trying to make a synthesis of things – Karl Marx, Mao,
as well as the drunk on the bar room floor. But most of it was talking about the relationships between people – my perceptions of them
– because that's what he was focused on – community; what is community? And the bits that held communities together were the connections between people.

I used to visit him on occasions, out at his centre, Continuing
Education, at the university. And at different times, when he was into

his cups, so to speak, talking about his own readings and understandings of community, he would read through and babble on about it and write about it. And the babbling, in a sense, was not unlike a set of tutorials about his understanding of the idea of community as written by some author from Germany or wherever. I remember particularly about the German author, can't remember his name, as he did a book review of it and he talked it through with me while he was reading it. So I was one of his talking posts – he used to talk a lot about his ideas with me.

It became a consistent thing over that time of '68. Mind you I was drawing my ideas from a lot of other sources and trying to connect them – although I wasn't conscious of doing that. But on reflection there was a consistent focus on sets of ideas – we'll call it broadly community. And what I was taking away from these discussions with Ned were the connections with what he was saying, to my experiences and understandings, as they were developing. For example – taking a conceptual idea such as community, and trying to say – well, where does that actually fit with the experiences that I have with different people?

And one of the key things he was talking about was change. How do you change the relationship so that it's more adaptive? And in turn that says – you can change this, if you both agree to talk about it, and take into account both parties' views on it – then, that changes everything. So I could make connections; with Jim Smith, or with my gang in Sydney – because we changed the world in our heads by talking to each other. So I understood, from all that, what could be talked about to negotiate change. So the idea of community adaptation made sense. It was very exciting.

The Aboriginal Human Relations Workshops

Ned aimed to focus on where you lived, and make changes there, as well as you being able to go to a different area and live in a changed world which you have helped form.

So his question, then, was how do you change, in that context? And that's where his particular approach was what he called Human Relations Workshops. Terrible bloody name! But, he maintained, you need, for a while, to act as though you are from another community, so to speak, and focus on the lived experience of being connected to each other and wanting to change. So you could talk about things that you would not otherwise talk about so explicitly in everyday life. So 'community', here, means those who came to these Human Relations Workshops. And we know community is a constructed thing, so you can have different experiences of it. So that's the main trick –to have a different experience. Because so much is habituated in our everyday life – the Ethels, the grandmas, the cousins – and there are only certain ways that you can talk with them that makes sense.

And Ned's model was derived, as well, from the therapeutic community – a psychiatric model. There was a colleague of Ned's called Neville Yeomans, who's since died. Neville had a very clear concept of recreating a community of relationships where the people in it, broadly speaking, were encouraged to change. We store the reality we experience here in our head or heart, and this is where we need to change in order to change in our outside world – and then we can change it in society.

So that was a marriage – Neville came along to these workshops to help with that idea of what we might now call *emotional choice*.

When he started these workshops Ned wanted to have males only – in a separate area – which was at the university in a hall with a living-in area, and for about ten days. Because, he reckoned, in his model of the world, that the blokes hadn't had much chance to talk, emotionally, realistically, as the women did. They had to do it every day: raising the kids and looking after each other; trying to organise the world around incompetent males. etc. He said – 'that's where the talk's missing. So focus on males; let them have a bit of a go; establish a reality that is commonly agreed upon; that'll just free up so much'. That was the idea. And it made sense to go about it that way.

Community activists

So for the next couple of years – two or three years in my experience – we did that. But we didn't just go along; this is when Ray Kelly started to come into the picture, because he was another one that Ned was talking to. And there was Ted Fields from Walgett[11]. Ned was looking for community activists – people who were aware, because of their practice, of what their experience of community was.

11   See discussion of Ned and the Aboriginal Human Relations Workshops in Ted's chapter on Ray Kelly; 'At last, someone else who understands' in Kijas J, 2005.

These community activists had been around before, but now they were coming into view in a different way post '67, as one realised the Welfare Board was going out of business. And even with the Sydney gang it was, 'you've got to talk to the community'. And that's where Ned realised that there are different sets of people to tap into. And he did social mapping of everyone – who drank with who – who got a lift with who etc. So he was as much a sociological modeller, as well as a practitioner of change, and this was the technique by which he'd try to do it. And it made sense. I could see that, because we could all relate it back to our everyday lives.

Final reflections

My life's been full of ever going change. But the constant has been the lessons learnt in earlier times – back in the late 60s, early 70s – from what Ned was on about, and still is on about in a slightly different way. with his Social Developers' Network. I retain that connection with Ned because, even though, as we all do, Ned's prone to babbling on, it's still a concerned view, and is derived from a constant idea of – '*that's* what's important' – 'yes, we should be doing more of *that*' – and then *he does it:* the social development, the idea of community, the negotiation of relationships.

Chapter 4

Working with the Grassroots

John Ducker

In the early days of Ned's work at UNE, he needed people who were interested in being involved in volunteer efforts on behalf of their communities. The interest of the Junior Chamber (JCs) in Inverell, where John Ducker, his cousin Graham Hughes and Doug Noone were leaders, was vital in the launch of a series of evolving community activities that Ned believed he could help foster and guide. He had recently decided to leave the practice of medicine and this was his first job in the new role he wanted to explore. Therefore it was very important that he succeed and John, Graham and Doug provided him with a key entry point.

Introducing John

I originated in Inverell and did my schooling there until I was 15, after which I became a jackaroo, trained as a wool classer and then worked in shearing sheds in many areas of the state, and beyond, for a number of years. In 1963 I was appointed as a teacher in TAFE and in 1964 was appointed in charge of the TAFE college at Inverell. I was promoted through several grades of principal and ended up in charge of Shellharbour college. After exiting the system. I've returned full circle to farming just outside of Temora.

The Inverell Study Development Group

Probably the story regarding Ned starts with the Inverell Regional Study Development Group. I think it was in 1966 that we conducted a seminar called 'Changing Social and Economic Roles of Rural Communities'. And from that seminar we selected – or a number of people got together afterwards – and we formed the Inverell Regional Study Development Group. That group undertook a number of projects. For example we instigated a survey of the area to assess the potential for industrial development, and the findings were used in later development. We also made a successful submission for the development of a national park in the area.

What made you interested in taking that community path?

In earlier days I came across a great diversity of people in the shearing sheds and in association with the community wherever I was working. And there was quite a lot of inequity – socially, work opportunities, all sorts of things – which were related back to the socio-economic background of the people concerned; particularly disadvantaged were the Aboriginal people. And that built in me a desire to do something for people, because there were lots who I thought deserved a lot better than they were getting.

Meeting Ned

When we organised the seminar it was through the JCs; a young persons group of 18s to 40s. I can't remember how we'd heard of Ned – but somebody with contact in the University of New England became aware of him and the role he was playing in the extensions department and we contacted him. So he sat in on the seminar. And then he was instrumental in helping us select the people that he thought would be beneficial for us to have in the group. That was our first introduction.

We met a man on that occasion who was obviously enormously dedicated to what he was doing – he was very concerned with social justice. He had in his mind ways in which things could be addressed to remedy what he saw as injustices and inequities, and in general to develop the communities he was having an association with. And that was happening through the self-help groups and the extension groups that he formed, such as ours.

The Bannockburn Conservation Group

Ned was influential with earlier advice. But our big project was the formation of the Bannockburn Conservation Group, which followed the other two I mentioned earlier. That really came as a result of the Study and Development group thinking about what were the major problems in the area. And one of them that we came up with was the prevalence of serious soil erosion. This was seen as a problem that would get worse unless something was done about it. So we took that on as a project.

There were a number of preliminary meetings between the Study Group and Ned as part of the planning that needed to be done to set up what we hoped would be a self-help group in the Bannockburn area. We had become familiar with the concept that the current methods, through the departmental agencies of soil conservation, had a number of inefficiencies in working only with individual farms. The ideal was to take a catchment area in total and plan its erosion control as a unit, even though there were lots of individual land holders. And this was the concept used with the Bannockburn Conservation Group. So our first work was to create an awareness in the people themselves: to get an admission, really, from them to themselves that they had an erosion problem.

So we constructed a survey that asked land holders things like the area of land they deemed to be suffering from erosion, and what they graded it as – mild to very severe etc. We gave people a fortnight to answer. We said we'd ring if we hadn't heard from them, and we got 100% coverage of the area. From that we had an indication who would be interested in attending a meeting later to discuss it all. After we collated the information we called a public meeting and invited various state government departments as well as some other interested individuals, and of course we endeavoured to get every one of the farmers in the Bannockburn catchment area. So that meeting was held.

Ned always maintained a very unobtrusive presence. He'd sit at the back of a meeting and not enter into the meetings at all – he'd simply observe. Then, after, he'd strategise the next steps with the group. In fact I can't remember Ned saying a word at the meetings. His input was enormously valuable and so was his unobtrusiveness – the people there hardly knew who Ned was. And that was part of the success.

If you'd come over the top and tried to extract from them what they needed to know too quickly, it may not have worked. They had to do that themselves. And that's what Ned strategised into happening.

It was very successful because we needed the cooperation of every farmer in that catchment area to make it work. Because, obviously, if someone in the centre said, 'No, I won't do it', then you couldn't really effectively do your water and soil conservation. We had a couple who were a bit tardy, but they came on board; peer pressure from fellow farmers. It took under a couple of years to produce results.

The Bannockburn Conservation Group went from strength to strength. They got expert knowledge from a farmer and wife retiring from the Darling Downs. That couple introduced new systems to the farmers, in particular the mulching of stubble instead of burning it. The Bannockburn farmers were able to increase their productivity and they diversified in an enormous number of things – pig raising and group insurance for example. They continued for a long, long while, until, as I later learned, it was only when there was an attempt made to take over the project by governmental and university authorities that the group said, 'Nope! we don't want that'. Otherwise I believe there would still be close cooperation there today – lives, cooperation, and productivity of the land.

Still networking

Soon after, late, '69, I was transferred to the Sydney region and lost contact with Ned, but there were members of the group who maintained that connection. One was a cousin of mine who passed away about two years ago, and Ned, from his archives, got my name and discovered my phone number, and, not knowing I was related to the person, rang me to tell me of his death. So it's been a lot of years. He is surely still doing his networking.

He's such a man that it was only about eight months ago at a Rotary Club meeting, and the guest speaker didn't turn up, so they said: 'we want three people to give a little talk about an outstanding Australian'. And I picked Ned. I primarily related his background as a medical doctor – flying doctor – till he realised most problems that were out there were social and not medical, so he changed his direction to where we came to know him.

Then I related our experience and the enormous influence he'd had with us. And I was aware of his self-help groups with Aboriginal people in Armidale and other areas. You know, the influence he had, as one person over such an enormous number of people, was fantastic, and the fact that that influence is still spreading is fantastic. There's not much change over those years in dedication, at all. His dedication hasn't waned one little iota – it's probably become more pronounced. I admire him greatly.

What did he do differently from what others were doing?

Primarily he worked, and had others work, from the grassroots level upward. It wasn't a top down project in any way at all. It was the people who were going to benefit who virtually helped themselves. It was a self-help project – an extremely well managed one – in which people were given the confidence and opportunity of doing something. And I think a lot of them were in the category of saying, 'It's not up to me. What can I do?' And Ned showed them that they could do what they did do. The confidence that he bestowed on a few, spread to a great number of people through their influence which followed.

Also I always found him very easy to work with. He had a very casual manner in his approach – even self-demeaning. In the time I was in Inverell I'd hear a voice down the corridor, 'Yahoo, is anyone at home'? And that would be Ned. We enjoyed that. We had a completely informal, relaxed relationship. Well, we had a friendship. It was a great experience for everyone who was in both those groups. He was a person you looked forward to seeing again.

Part Three

Social Developers' Network

Chapter 5

Tag Team: Establishing SDN

John Russell

Community Development focus

I live in Melbourne but was born and educated in country NSW. In 1964 I went to the University of NSW where I did a social work course and became interested in community development (CD). I was influenced by Tony Vinson, one of my lecturers, and by reading articles about current innovative change programs under the "War on Poverty" in the USA. CD is a subset of social work, but most social workers don't do community development – most do case work. Prior to a visit to New Guinea in 1966, I had perceived Australians as generally egalitarian. However I was shocked when I observed how badly the majority of Australians employed in the colonial administration at that time, treated the local population. I then became interested in the application of CD in developing countries, and subsequently studied in India for 2 years, (1978-79).

In 1969 I became the first social worker with South Sydney Community Aid, funded through the Department of Immigration. We opened a shop front in Redfern – connected with the Good Neighbour Council. It was a community based organisation, initiated by local ministers of the United Church. Also on the Management Committee were 2 prominent aldermen of the Labor-controlled South Sydney

Municipal Council. I started as a lone worker and was able to develop a range of citizen-based CD programs. I was also able to assist in the establishment of the Aboriginal Medical and Legal Services.

I moved to Melbourne in 1971 and worked as a CD officer in the Broadmeadows housing commission area, funded by the Brotherhood of St Lawrence. When the Whitlam Government introduced the Australian Assistance Plan (AAP) I became the Social Planner for the much larger North-West Melbourne Region. The AAP facilitated a wide range of CD programs and this was stimulated by Ned and I running a SDN workshop at Stockton (near Newcastle), specifically for CD workers employed under the AAP.

Hitting it off

As the final practical placement of my course, I spent 4 months visiting Southeast Asian countries looking at CD programs. I returned in 1968 via Darwin and Alice Springs and then went to an ACOSS conference in Queensland – (Australian Council of Social Services). One of the speakers was Ned Iceton. I spoke to him afterwards and he invited me to meet up with him in Armidale, on my way back to Sydney. I spent a few days and he took me out to the local Aboriginal settlement. We had a good rave about CD and social change issues. We found we were on the same wave length and that was the start of my long term involvement with Ned.

Ned had issues with his employer – he always had them with the University of New England. When we first started the social development workshops, that was one of Ned's regular themes. He used the workshops as a sounding-off board for all the problems he was having with the bureaucracy of the university because they had a particularly limited view of what they thought CD should be. He thought that one reason he got the job at Armidale was because he had Dr with his name and that gave status to the department.

Giving a push: the first workshop

Ned talked to me about the Aboriginal workshops he'd been doing and how it might be worthwhile to transpose that type of workshop into the wider community. I supported that, but he seemed to lack enough drive to get it off the ground. My role with Ned was to push him to actually do it, on the basis we would be doing it together. It goes without saying, that we were very pleased with the result, but the concept was Ned's.

I admired Ned because of his exceptional conceptual analysis and his easy verbal articulation. He was less confident in putting his insights in writing. He was also unusual in his ability to analyse both from the personal (micro) to the global (macro). He consistently advocated for the inter-relationship of both. It was very important for the SDN workshops to deal with both. An important element was to recognise and meet (as far as possible), individual needs. I maintain that the SDN is the only mechanism I am aware of, capable of holistically assisting an individual to deal with any CD issue!

We held the first workshop, probably in Morisset (NSW), Ned thinks in 1975. I think it was earlier. Most of the people there were people that Ned had connections with. I don't recall recruiting anyone. There were about a dozen people and everyone seemed to think it worked very well! It went for about a week – all our first ones went for 6 or 7 days, which was the Aboriginal workshop model. It was quite exhausting but invigorating and good.

Tag team

Ned and I worked as a kind of tag team – we developed this as we went along. Ned was the intellectual who did the head work, talked about the theory and looked at the process. I did not talk much but was the one who could sometimes tune into people's emotions and who interrupted the process when I thought there was a sensitive area which should be checked out. That's how I saw the workshops; Ned and I both contributing in different ways. In the early days, we refined the process as we went along. It also did not take long for leadership to be shared within the group and for Ned and me to take a backseat for much of the time.

We compiled an agenda at the start, giving everyone who wanted it a time-slot to discuss something of concern to them. Later on we introduced a 'creative listening' session as a prelude to the agenda. These days I am probably more active and Ned now takes a back role completely. I get anxious if things don't start on time and I sometimes try to draw out issues. Most of the time I stay quiet if I feel satisfied that things are going nicely. If I feel uneasy about something I may join in the discussion. Sometimes that can be facilitating and sometimes not. I'm not sure – my insight about that is probably biased.

We developed a system of having sessions that were based on the work that people were doing in the community. And that was mixed up with people's personal hassles and problems. It was what Ned would say was the 'yin and the yang'. People were at different stages. Some were more absorbed with their personal problems at the time, which interfered – meant they couldn't give much time to outside and community change issues. Then they'd come back next year and they would have solved their personal stuff and they were into the community stuff. People who came regularly did that from time to time.

Early workshops

The workshops in the first few years tended to be more confrontational. I was part of that. If I picked up some inauthenticity that I thought was going on, at the emotional rather than the intellectual level, then I tended to challenge people. So we had a few emotional sessions.

Because Ned talked a lot, people who had anti-authoritarian tendencies projected that onto Ned, although he wasn't particularly that way as I saw him. Because he was very much a theoretician and the workshops were very much a vehicle for Ned to talk about issues as he saw them, he talked about insights that he was working on at the time – and I thought that was good. But he didn't always know when to stop talking, so people tended to stop listening if he went on too long. That tended to be one of the issues.

It took Ned quite a long time to modify his style but that was OK. But if somebody else came with very strong views or personality, which happened occasionally, then sometimes the workshops could end up being a debate between Ned and the other person, until someone else did something about it. It was all grist for the mill.

Evolution of the workshops

I thought we had a good blend of a range of issues. As different people came we developed. The workshops were presented as self-help and anybody could assume leadership or provide scripts.

That evolved right from the beginning because I think Ned and I were clear that while we might try to facilitate, neither of us had any particular ego need to be in control or dominating.

It was interesting – when Ned met Joan it was quite good for Ned as he felt more settled and Joan made major contributions to the group. She was able to bring more focus on feelings and emotions.

The first workshops, looking back, where probably too male centred. There were always females in the group and some weren't necessarily submissive! There were plenty who could stand up and speak for themselves. But there was a regular theme in workshops where one or more of the women would focus on gender issues and try to make sure there wasn't a totally male perspective or bias. So we did go through a feminism phase while we were having workshops, but I don't remember it being a major issue. There were a couple of prominent women around, Joan McCarthy comes to mind – she's still around. She played an important role in producing the SDN newsletter.

Confrontation still occurs but it's done in a more caring way. And it's done in a way that people can accept and not close down – not feel put upon. That did come about as a change in the group – a positive change. It evolved as people developed skills. And if people were too confrontational they got sat on. I think as women became more active in the group, it has helped SDN gain a more caring way of doing things. This has been demonstrated by women being more creative in running their sessions. The most memorable SDN session I have ever participated in was a clown workshop. More recently it would seem to me that workshops are becoming more focused on global issues rather than personal, i.e.; the 'macro' rather than the 'micro'. It could be argued that global issues are becoming more important, but I also think that the tendency for the majority of participants to be male is also a factor.

A trusted sounding board

It's not easy to explain to someone what an SDN workshop is! I would say that it's an opportunity for anyone interested in social change, or wanting to influence their community, to get support. Also if they aren't sure if the way they want to do it is the best way – well they can come and use SDN as a sounding board. They can get positive reinforcement in most cases, but they can get challenged if it appears they may be unaware of some aspect of what they're doing that might adversely affect some people they're working with.

One of the other benefits of SDN is that people are able to develop a high degree of trust in a fairly short time. Otherwise people will have difficulty accepting what could be seen as negative feedback. I think that's one reason we can work on our three or four day basis now instead of seven days, because we can be effective. In the early workshops it took a couple of days before people felt they could trust each other and talk openly, whereas now, right from day one, people can talk fairly openly and people who come for the first time can have a sense that it's OK to talk and they'll be listened to and supported. That's why we can help people with personal problems as well. It's much quicker now because trust already exists between the majority of participants who have attended previous workshops. Trust also develops much quicker when the workshops are residential.

That's a big change – or is it an evolution?

Workshops are continually evolving and always need a range of people with different skills. They've been honed over time. The ideal number of participants is around a dozen and we have fixed a maximum of 18.

One of my theories in community development is that you need people who will polarise things. So if you want to bring about social change you need someone who can articulate the ideal and then there needs to be some push to move towards that. There need to be others who can resolve the potential conflict, mediate, compromise and through that there will be an improvement on what existed before.

I see each workshop as different and there will always be highlights, issues and problems, but on the whole I think we resolve them. The strength of the workshops is that whatever issues come up, are dealt with in productive ways. I think at the end of the workshop almost everybody goes away saying, "This has been a very useful process."

People can come to a workshop and not participate particularly, but in most cases they will be gaining from the discussions. What often happens is that one person's issue will trigger insights in another participant. They may then work on it, go away and apply it later or talk to someone outside of the group.

There are strengths in everybody and people will generally rise to the occasion as requires. There seems to be some kind of osmosis. Generally speaking we're successful because the leadership can change, and people can contribute and help resolve the situation. We've got a range of skilled people who come to the workshops and they offer a wide range of approaches. We can always find something that will suit the particular situation. That's one of our strengths, so that we are not stuck on a particular way of handling a situation.

Annual and local workshops

In the early days in Victoria we started having workshops because that was where I was. We also involved people through the Australian Assistant Plan (AAP) during the Whitlam period which were the halcyon days for community development workers, so we had workshops near Melbourne and they went well. We've had them in a number of places – Sydney, NSW North Coast and Canberra. Ned is on top of that. But we developed a pattern of yearly workshops, which at that stage were held in Armidale. Then later we developed the pattern of alternating them between Armidale or Melbourne – or places close by. At the early regional workshops, either Ned or Michael might come, but later we operated independently. We held a number of Victorian ones at Mt Baw Baw.

It's interesting that the SDN hasn't particularly built up its members – but it hasn't withered on the vine either.

One of the recurring questions is what will happen to SDN when Ned can't carry on that networking role. What are your thoughts?

I think we'll still have workshops in Melbourne, but it will depend on who we can find, or fund, to try and replace Ned. But Ned's hard to replace because of his networking ability. I also link people in and so do others. But it's the difficulty with all organisations as their membership ages that they aren't being replaced by younger people. There certainly isn't the idealism amongst the younger people that there was in my day – I graduated from university in 1968.

Members

Is there a pattern of people who came back or didn't?

I'm not good at that sort of analysis. There were lots who have kept coming. I've probably been to most. People like Joan McCarthy were very instrumental for a long time and then moved out, but others moved in. People self-selected. I don't think there's been a great deal of change to how things have worked over time. But it works partly because there's a core of people who come – ideally half the people should be new and half returning people. The reality is the majority are returning people. There are usually a minimum number of ten. People come because of word of mouth. They come because they've been recommended rather than reading about it. We've made attempts to publicise them without much success.

I've always been paid in my line of CD work until I retired at age 70 – I've been lucky. At least half or more who came to these workshops weren't employed in CD work, so they were volunteer community activists. The beauty and benefit of SDN, compared to a lot of other groups, was that it is not biased towards any professional grouping or any particular coterie of persons. Everybody is welcome.

There wasn't much of an ethnic mix – basically Anglo-Saxon. Ned tried to get some Aboriginal people to come to workshops, but only lately has had success. There weren't many migrants. But we've had a wide range of people come with a social justice/left wing focus. We've had people who've come with a strong spiritual feeling, or 'new age' focus, people working on environmental issues, people coming from an alternative culture in terms of various collectives – North Coast communes, doctors, psychiatrists, a range of professionals, as well as housewives and farmers – people who are active in the community.

A commitment to social justice

What's common with everyone in SDN is that they have a basic commitment to a social justice orientation – wherever they get it from. There are lots of other groups that many of us belong to who also have that at their core.

So is there something unique about SDN?

Well, it's unique in that it's the only organisation I know that deals with issues at both the intellectual and emotional level. It's also non-discriminatory in terms of who participates, as long as they have this common theme of commitment to social justice and what people identify as positive social change.

Chapter 6

No Longer a Lone Peg

Sylvia Baker

From engineering to social development

I live in Deniliquin. Our rural population is about 8,000 people and the total population of the rural shires that focus into us is around 23,000. We arrived in about 1952. It was a personal decision to move out of Melbourne. We had a child with an illness who needed to be over the mountain range into a drier climate. The sun seemed to shine all the time in the Murray Valley, and Deniliquin didn't have an engineer. My husband was an engineer, and my own engineering background was in the electrical field. I thought I could work from home on a consulting basis.

I soon came up against a number of issues where I realised that most of the women had no conception of where they stood in society. None of their issues fed into local government. We found we'd come from a totally different culture. It was rather disconcerting at first, but the people were so great. So prior to meeting Ned there was this social issues stuff, and I found myself moving from engineering to social development.

To me there was a dreadful social injustice in the town over the price of bread. It was more expensive than the whole of New South Wales, as far as I could see. It was being sold at the delivery price in the shops, but there was no delivery. Women had to make a long walk into town to get the bread. And when I asked, 'what will we do about

it', people said, 'well, we can't do anything'. I said we'd have a public meeting, which we held in the local tennis club and we couldn't fit
everyone in! I was quite shocked by the number that turned up, but it
was a community issue – everyone depended on bread. That was the
catalyst that brought me into an active role in the community.

Then there was a bi-election for council and I got in. There started
a new life of complete involvement in community life. I really enjoyed
what I was doing, but I found it difficult at times with three small children. In those days I don't think there was such a thing as a babysitter
to hire. But I had a very good friend – she had 11 children – and she
looked after mine every time I had a committee meeting. Wonderful
support! I couldn't have managed without that. I used to feel that
every woman I met in the local government world had a social con-
science, but I couldn't say that about every male member of councils!
All the women were on the social development level, doing something
for their community. There weren't many women at that time in local
government, anywhere. I think there were about 36 in the whole of
Australia.

On the path to meeting Ned

So I had a passion for community development, because the people
seemed so neglected, it seemed to me. They had no information. They
knew nothing about the welfare stuff they could access. It wasn't getting through to them. And I don't know where the churches were who
were supposed to have some pastoral care for their parishioners.

Then through what we called our 'total aged care committee' we
became the Regional Social Development Council, based in Deniliquin
at that time. And the Regional Social Development Council was forming at the same time that the Whitlam government was forming the
Australian Assistance Plan and I thought – oh heavens, here's a seren-
dipity thing. This is something we've been waiting for. And the AAP
was a whole-of-Australia thing; I thought we should be in that. It was
a movement that seemed to be swooping across the whole countryside.
And it was at that time that Ned was forming his social development
structure. I think he says the first workshop he had was '75 or '74.
And he heard of our council for social development way down on the
southern border and got in contact with us.

Prior to that contact, he'd led a delegation to China and through the Social Workers Union, of which I became a member. They had in their newsletter this mention of people being invited to tour China. Ned led that delegation. (And it was in this time that Whitlam had gone to China to open up relation). Two of us represented the regional areas on that delegation – me from Deniliquin and a man from Daylesford in Victoria. So that's when I first came into contact with Ned.

However, in Deniliquin at that time, I had an Aboriginal lass work- ing with me who acted as a liaison officer with the Aboriginal peo- ple and that was Jenny, David [Crew's] wife[12]. She was only young then. And she was in touch with Ned through some Aboriginal stud- ies group that he was running. So there was another connection with Deniliquin. I remember helping Jenny with some of the stuff that came through on that newsletter of Ned's. And I might even have written something – although I didn't meet him until the Chinese delegation.

In Ned I found someone who was so easy to talk to, who had exactly the same thoughts as me. I wasn't a lone peg out there on the clothes line. And it was really Ned that gave me the impetus for my local government and community work, because he understood what I was on about at a time when I really couldn't articulate it. It was his personality and the way we clicked. And he mentioned that this social development group was being set up and suggested I might be inter- ested. And I was – very!

The SDN workshops

I probably started when we came back from that first trip to China – perhaps it was 1978 or 79. I think they'd already had some meetings by that time.

I really did need to come because I felt it always gave me new energy to carry on what I was doing. But in order to get to them I had to make some odd arrangements! My friend Molly would look after the children in the daytime and my husband would collect them and look after them at night. My husband would have to drive me to a town about 70 km away for me to catch the train, which would take all afternoon and night, and arrive in Sydney the next morning; then another train to Armidale – so it would take me two days to get there. Another time I found a bus that came through Deniliquin to Dubbo

---

12   See David's reflections in chapter ten.

– then a change to Armidale. Ned would meet me and take me home for a shower, and then we'd get to the meeting. The first time I came to Armidale was to 'the flats', as they called them, attached to the university. It was in holiday time.

I found a very stimulating round of discussions, all focused on social development, which I became vitally interested in. I couldn't talk about these things in my own home area, because people didn't understand what I was on about. It was in the process of developing something that gave me satisfaction. But the stimulation for the workshops came from meeting with a group of like-minded people – and that was the Social Development Network. And to know that there were other people around that I could contact. I contacted Ned, but I also contacted John in Melbourne and someone else in Ballarat, and someone in Bendigo and so on, if I wanted to. That sort of connection was wonderful. So that became the way I worked.

I made it my business to do that. And to me, every year that I met with the network – and Ned in particular because he was always there – collectively the energy that was accumulated in that particular spot reinvigorated me to the extent, and gave me tremendous impetus, to continue with what I could see was a social developmental process – building social capital in my own community. So through that, at last, I'd found the key. That was the impression that I had.

I think the workshops have always been successful, from a personal point of view. The format works. There would be some perfectionists for whom it wouldn't work – someone needing a strategic plan for example. And a pattern does come through – but it's not a planned one. There's a good gender balance and we've had some people from different backgrounds – Indians, Chinese, Ethiopians. I can't always come but I still keep in contact – so there's a continual linkage into the network which is valuable indeed.

Changes and continuity

I have seen changes. In the early days there was a lot of personal development going on between the people who were involved in social, and or community development. And I think that people who were in that field needed to know what they themselves were on about. And that came through very largely because of Ned's wife Joan, who was a bit like Beth Basnett (now known as Cariad Duff) –their field was education of some sort – and were able to flesh out a lot of personal problems, personal growth. Learning curves became apparent; you knew your journey from here to there and you were able to follow it through.

Now, it seems to me that it's broadened tremendously, because each of us is working in specific fields. When we come together like this, each year, we learn a bit more about different aspects of the involvement of the different participants and thus we learn from personal experience. And people give it so freely – it's wonderful to be able to pick up on their experiences and apply it to our own. And that way we learn tremendously, I think. It's a four day session with social development people, and always within the presence of Ned and John; they seem to me to be the catalysts in the SDN movement.

I'd like to see the format that has evolved within our loose network structure continue, because I think we get more from it. The format that I see is that we all get together in the circle – I see that as important – and we list the things we need to talk about, so we form a pretty loose agenda in a timeframe that suits us. I think it's important that we have our meals together, lunch and dinner, because that seems to bind the group in the time we are here. So I'd like to see SDN continue, but we need funding to see that happen. And in the next few years we'll come up with funding. I'm sure we'll find a way to establish this as a permanent operation within our society.

And that goes beyond the lynch pin of Ned?

Yes.

Ned

He has a charisma I guess – but he also has a lot of energy. And he was able to enunciate all the complexities that I knew very little about, and bring them into a logical pattern that I could discern and apply to my particular locality.

Where do you think Ned's knowledge came from?

Well part of it was from his own personal growth and development, but of course he was a very intellectual person, and was in fact lecturing in this subject at the UNE. And I guess I saw that as a learning curve for me – so I tapped into his knowledge bank.

What was the learning curve that you refer to?

That there was all this literature out there that I knew nothing about. Because I wasn't trained in social development – it was just something that hit me as being a necessary thing in the community in which I found myself. And I'd been searching for it for a long time – and I found it – and Ned was the catalyst that brought that about.

On his journeys around the state Ned would make a point of contacting me. We became quite good friends – he and his wife. And each time I came through Armidale, I always called. I talked to him on the phone, wrote letters, and now we have email. He has remained a very staunch ally, confidant, support person, mentor – the whole thing. Any time I have problems in the social development work I'm doing, then I always contact him. We talk about it and we flesh it out and usually we find a solution.

I've always found him extremely easy to talk to. We're on the same wavelength. I find him, sometimes, a bit pedantic, but always with a sense of humour, so it doesn't become a ritual-kind of thing. And I think his own knowledge of himself is so good that he can appreciate where we're coming from when we're talking to him – and integrate his thoughts with those that are coming from other sources. He's a particularly good friend, and I think that friendship goes right throughout the whole group. So he's a great people person – really great.

The network

It's a very loose organisation. Everyone has become very close friends. We've almost become a unit in its own right, and while it's very loosely organised the network is still there, and we can be in constant touch with one another. We aren't, necessarily. But if there's a problem within our various fields of interest, we can always find someone in the network to talk to. And that someone will always listen and be helpful. And I think that's a tremendous plus in any organisation.

Chapter 7

Community Development and SDN

Ben Leeman

Introducing Ben

I'm 64 years old and although since 1960 I lived mostly in Melbourne, my accent is not Australian. My birthplace, the Netherlands, remains a special place for me. Whilst I would like to see myself more as a world citizen, I'm an Australian by choice. Born during the Second World War into a large working class family provided both opportunities and challenges. Religion divided my large extended family. That drove me to explore different religious denominations as well as finding joy in humanistic philosophy. Searching for God, but also earnestly seeking answers how war, and the killing and destruction it involved, but also how extreme poverty and racial discrimination, could be justified, drove my search for enlightenment.

We were too poor for me to go to high school, but as I liked books I was encouraged to learn a printing trade. When my eldest brother was called-up for the then compulsory national service into the Dutch military it became crunch time for me. Successful job applications, one to South Africa and the other to Dutch New Guinea (West Irian) were vetoed – too dangerous! Persistence however paid off. My parents reluctantly allowed me to leave home at 18 and granted me permission to travel alone – with lots of other immigrants – to Australia. On arrival, my printing qualifications were not recognised in Melbourne.

Instead, I obtained a job at General Motors whilst seeking to obtain permission to complete the final three years apprenticeship as a compositor, as one had to be 21 to be a tradesman.

Living in St Kilda and volunteering for a Catholic charity exposed me to a wide range of social problems and my inability 'to make a difference'. Discontentment with my job as a compositor encouraged me to further my education. I was keen to increase my knowledge about resolving individual and social problems hence I resolved to study social work. That necessitated completing high school. In the Netherlands I had left school at grade 7 (a completed apprenticeship does not count). Luckily the Victorian education system allowed mature entry into year 12, and after two years of evening studies I matriculated in 1966. A year or so earlier I had met Elizabeth and we married on the last day of 1966, after which we travelled to Ceylon and India, before visiting my family after an absence of 7 years and then on to Mexico – to visit Elizabeth's sister – before returning to Australia.

From 1968 to 1972 I enjoyed my studies in social work and sociology (at honours level) at the University of NSW. Involvement included representing students on the Faculty Board.

I left university after five years without graduating due to family and financial pressures, but also because feeling unsure about becoming a graduate, which to me creates a barrier between the have and have-nots.

My parents' marriage had broken down, and my father, depressed and feeling lost, accepted my invitation to come and stay with us in Sydney in June 1972, my final year at university. My own marriage was also on the rocks. Although Elizabeth and I had separated, Elizabeth was expecting our second child and expressed a preference to stay in Sydney. However in 1970, having obtained a bursary from the Alexander Home and Hospital for the Aged ($15 pw plus university fees) I was bonded to my first social work job at the Alexander in Castlemaine Victoria and started work there in November 1972. A month later Elizabeth joined us there and our second child was born in February 1973. Six weeks later Elizabeth decided to return to Sydney, wishing to continue her nursing training and wanting to take our two children with her. Together we travelled to Sydney, found accommodation and a family to care for our children.

My father's cancer of the oesophagus worsened and he refused surgery, expecting to die in Australia. Then in May 1973 my father changed his mind and decided to return to the Netherlands where he was admitted to a hospital on arrival and died ten days later at the age of 63 shocking my three brothers and two sisters. Being in debt and bonded to my employer, isolated with no family nearby and few close friends, I could not afford to accompany him, something I regret to this day.

After leaving the Alexander I successfully obtained a job in local government (the City of Sunshine) with the ageing. This enabled me to develop my interests and skills in community development, both in a paid and voluntary capacity. Working a 9-day fortnight made it possible for me to visit my children in Sydney every two weeks, but concern about childcare arrangements continued to grow. Another social worker, and fellow founding committee member of ECCV, the Ethnic Communities' Council of Victoria, Jean[(my future partner), joined me on regular visits to Sydney and readily bonded with my two children. In 1976, together with Jean and the two children, we visited the Netherlands to see my mother and extended family. Thereafter the two children stayed with us in Melbourne. A few years later Jean and I married and added two more children to the two of my first marriage.

In 1979, following Jean's encouragement, I finally graduated in social work at Melbourne University. Further formal education included graduate studies in Rehabilitation Studies in 1983 and in Human Services Evaluation Research in 1987. Jobs included local government community work and medical social work as well as volunteer work within the Victorian Dutch community. For twenty years I worked in different capacities within the Commonwealth Rehabilitation Service with people who have a disabling condition and especially with people from a non Anglo-Celtic background. The ADEC (Action on Disabilty in Ethnic Communities), which I helped set up in collaberation with two severely disabled people, awarded me with life membership. In 2004, in recognition of my 40 years of involvement in voluntary work I was awarded a scholarship for a PhD in volunteering research by Victoria University.

Invited to participate in a SDN workshop

In the late 1960s at the University of NSW I met John Russell and we have been friends ever since. John invited me to join the Aboriginal interest group of the Australian Association of Social Workers of which

he was the convener whilst I was the university's local Abschol director (a student fundraising charity for Aboriginal scholarships). John
also invited me to come to my first SDN meeting in Armidale in 1975.
From that date I've participated in most SDN workshops. I've missed
a couple due to other commitments.

It is important for me to attend those SDN workshops as they are
challenging, invigorating and attended by experienced community
activists. The workshops are guided by the thoughtful and insightful
comments of Ned Iceton and facilitated by John Russell and Michael
Maher. Sylvia Baker, David Purnell, Mary Porter, Beth Basnett and
others bring vastly different experiences and extensive knowledge to
the workshops. The sharing of personal experiences, often challenging,
and the discussion which generates from their presentations enriches
the workshops and provides food for thought and stimulation for
ongoing activism. We all are challenged at times by Ned Iceton's, Beth
Bassnett's and Jean Leeman's concerns for social justice and equality.
As a group we welcome new participants, their comments and ques-
tioning, as most of us realize that SDN needs to grow and increase
the number of workshop participants. Ned is also keen that the SDN
members conduct additional workshops, a wish that has only partially
been fulfilled.

Why SDN?

At university and within social work there were lots of opportunities
for discussions and workshops and sharing ideas with colleagues. Yet
the SDN workshops provided a different type of challenge. Listening
– having the opportunity to explain the work we were doing, but also
receiving feedback without being judged about whether we are doing
the right thing. Rather, one received feedback in a positive and developmental way, how things could be done differently. Frequently this
involved exploring suggestions and ways of trying to develop alternative goals whilst working towards a fairer and more humane society, discussing ways of overcoming the political limitations; and also
becoming personally more able to cope with the uncertainties and
frustration inherent in community work, with expert support from
others who are not directly involved. The focus on developing emotional intelligence is a key element in the SDN workshops, and Ned

Iceton's perseverance in exploring and promoting that form of under-standing and the praxis energy it generates form a core part of SDN's philosophy.

Emotional Intelligence

Few people have read, meditated, networked and discussed as much as Ned Iceton, or to put it more precisely, few people have devel-oped over many years an inner growth, augmenting his intellectual ability with emotional intelligence. Ned promotes and utilizes emo-tional intelligence as it enhances not just clear thinking, but also one's effectiveness.

In a SDN workshop discussions are confidential. Personal stories shared are to stay in the room. People present particular experiences, ideas and opinions. Some are personal success stories, others are less so, and may be painful, but often contain important insights based upon actual lived experiences. It doesn't mean these presentations are neutral or objective – participants have their value viewpoints, but they are also willing to share insights from which others can learn. The other workshop participants aren't there to say whether you are a good worker or have the skills or the right attitudes, but rather – how can you do things more effectively. We can learn from one another's community development practice. It enhances personal effectiveness as well as enabling you to work differently, more effectively through applying the experience of others. Whilst most of the discussions are praxis and existentially based, sometimes a comment is made about a useful reference. For instance, one of Ned's favoured books is *M. Mitchell Waldrop* **Complexity: The Emerging Science at the Edge of Order and Chaos.**

Sharing deep personal experiences, projects or activities that turned out differently from what was expected can be exasperating. Sharing experiences about a negative personal relationship is never easy, even with people one trusts and respects. Only in a few workshops has a participant become emotional and briefly cried often as the result of a cathartic release. Being able to share deep intimate feelings and unre-solved personal issues amongst a group of trusted and respected peo-ple can be exhilarating but also provides situations where emotions can no longer be fully controlled. To cry in a support group such as a SDN workshop enables a few participants to release pent-up emotions, sharing the pain and negative thoughts about it and move on, enriched by the experience of being heard and understood by others. Therefore to me, the emotional stuff, that is not the issue. But what was important was the humanity coming through – the concern for others in the discussions. And that can be emotional – and we share that – the thoughtfulness of so many members who want to work towards creating a better world where human rights are important. Another participant may present a success story, the hard and at times frustrating work has paid off, and that joy is celebrated and the presenter congratulated. Sometimes the community development process used in a presentation is analysed: can that approach be used in other situations?

This is done in a supported and moderated discussion covering a whole range of topics we are personally deeply involved in – political, social, as well as economic, and personal experiences.

The SDN Network is a group of people who are prepared to listen to what each one wants to discuss and provide some feedback – not to judge but to support and to facilitate. The participants are from a wide variety of backgrounds, but all share a concern for others. Most don't have a barrow to push, or if they do, that becomes less important because it is the group dynamics that will determine the focus and direction of the discussion. Our individual endeavours are to work towards a more humane and socially just world and that ought to begin with changing ourselves and developing our understanding of the theory and practice of community work. SDN guiding principles promote that understanding and provide possibly a unique basis for mutual support. That makes the workshops different from other personal growth and action-oriented planning groups. SDN members learn from one another and provide support and invaluable insights.

Most of the SDN members are very committed people who are prepared to put themselves out for others or for a particular cause. If that view or experience is not shared, that can, at times, be difficult as they are willing to listen to others but also to provide honest feedback without too many fears of being judged. Therefore to put one's own ideas, positive and negative experiences, on the line, is to expose oneself. Yes, one can be vulnerable, but mostly participants remain comfortable in the group due to knowing that the group is supportive – and that the guidelines under which the group operates, such as strict confidentiality and not interrupting, provide some sense of trust and enable the participants to identify with one another. Yet, at times, it is hard not to be judgmental and we do not always succeed. Some of the learning experience is indirect and perhaps not fully understood until much later. As a consequence many new workshop participants attend only once whilst a core group of less than twenty come from time to time, and about half, almost always.

Community Development and SDN

SDN philosophy is based upon the knowledge that people are capable of achieving extra-ordinary things through the application of emotional intelligence, mutual support and persistence. Resilience is strengthened through workshop participation and further developed through the networking SDN encourages. Seeding funding from the NED-Net (such as attending/participating in a conference on '*Restorative Justice*', providing core funding for an Indigenous Australian regional workshop, the seed funding to re-commence the publication of '*New Community Quarterly*' Australia's only community development journal and in many other ways) has enabled SDN to make significant contributions to community development. And all this is done with Ned's private funds without government assistance or tax deductibility – and without publicity or public recognition.

SDN is not based in a particular academic discipline: it's based much more or less on received wisdom, existential feelings, wide experience, lots of readings and network discussions with lots of people together with a deep concern for others less well-off and in receiving and giving feedback based upon years of practice. New ideas, innovative books and ideas are readily shared and these cover a wide range of issues and topics and are not limited to texts on community development. Thus SDN, without a strong theoretical community development underpinning, does not have a particular academically recognised theory or practice. It is not based upon a particular set of theory or practice. Instead it is broadly based, enabling anyone to participate and contribute without having to be familiar with the language, theory and practice of that particular broadly based academic subject. For some it is based on life experience facilitated by networking and learning from one another and through reflection. For others it is linked to previous study, paid work and voluntary community involvement.

SDN is similar to a social movement and is not an academic discipline. It is personal growth and community action oriented. It aims to enhance the effectiveness of individual praxis. It encourages participants to be creative and innovative: to be a change agent. Therefore SDN is not prescriptive, encourages action and is supportive of social development projects in a very wide field.

Ben's views about Ned, SDN and the N.E.D. Foundation

I admire Ned for his perseverance, his concern for others, his intellect and his conceptual ability to perceive other ways of looking at things. He has an interesting conceptual ability to go to the heart of the matter and the desire to share these insights with others. At other times I feel he is too focused on one thing without seeing the broader picture. He has developed a challenging approach – never taking anything for granted as there are many ways of understanding a situation. But at times he appears to have a somewhat pessimistic view to certain global issues that I don't find helpful. I think, to be successful as a community developer, you have to have an optimistic outlook. Sure, one needs to be realistic and pragmatic, but also idealistic and having confidence in the future. And also in oneself. As an individual thinker, often going against the grain of popular opinion and conservative Australian government policies as well as global economic and social policies, demands enormous resilience and confidence. Ned gives a great deal of himself and of his resources. And what does Ned receive in return? Living alone for many years, he has developed a routine focusing on encouraging others to become change agents and continues to set examples. That is a demanding role for which he is not fully appreciated. Ned appears not to seek social rewards or public recognition, but would like to be understood and supported in his main goals and endeavours to work toward a fairer and more humane society.

It does bother me that SDN is not better known. What does concern me is where will SDN and the N.E.D. Foundation go after Ned dies? It is true that, as Ned says, he is now 'only a participant' within the workshop. However before the workshop, for the whole year, he is actually continually promoting workshops, together with assistance from Michael Maher and through contact with other Board members. But there is a whole informal 'one to one' network that keeps Ned going. So there is such a lot that goes on outside the workshops which is not only important for Ned but also for all SDN members.

Ned Iceton is a true altruist. He is hoping that the N.E.D. Foundation of SDN, through obtaining charitable status, will be able to continue the work he has pioneered throughout his lifetime. It deserves to be achieved.

Dr Ned Iceton is a true Australian innovator and public intellectual, a giant who challenges all of us to follow his footsteps, or at least use our own emotional energy to implement the wisdom and goals of *Nurturing Evolutionary Development*.

Chapter 8

Fair Feedback in Critical Reflection

Tiyana Maksimovic-Binno

Meeting Ned

I'm originally from Yugoslavia, Belgrade. My Iraqi husband and I wanted to settle there, but he could not get a permanent residence without getting a job, and vice versa. So we lived in Iraq, then in Algeria, where we could both get work, as town and regional planners. But having moved several times with our two children was very unsettling and taxing. At the end of 1985, when I was 38, we migrated to Australia, to start a new life as permanent residents, supposedly with good employment opportunities. Instead, prospective employers said that we have been overqualified and unemployable without local experience. Under such pressure, within few months our marriage broke up, and I hit a huge midlife crisis. Without personal support whatsoever, I became a deeply depressed sole parent of two, marginalized, disempowered, debilitated and totally disillusioned with mainstream and my own path to 'success'. I started desperately looking for alternatives in all respects, and especially needed to heal myself from having been deluded to accept the mainstream views and lifestyle. Instead, I wanted to recover my original Pristine Self, but did not know how.

At that stage I met Ned, at the beginning of 1987, at Schumacher's memorial conference[13]. After hearing my presentation about a project for an alternative, environmentally and also emotionally sustainable and healing urban household-community, Ned invited me to attend the Social Developers' Network (SDN) week-long workshop in Armidale. Like Ned, I perceived illness as socially-based before being microbe-induced, so I was delighted to find out that he had the same insight, and that SDN was a community of like-minded people – just what I was looking for since I did not have my proper place in Australia, and did not want to even try to fit any more into the mainstream. Therefore Ned and I had an instant good personal connection, and I liked and appreciated him very much. I went to my first workshop-soon after, with my new partner and my children.

Remembering the SDN workshops

I found that workshop fantastic – it was high quality, friendly and cheap. Still in crisis, I was very poor, living on sole parent's pension, and could not afford any extras. So I appreciated that being at the workshop did not cost much more than being at home. Living on the UNE campus, we catered for ourselves, which was good fun too, and participants presented all workshops free of charge. I was also greatly relieved to realise that other participants, who held jobs as counsellors, teachers etc., were personally in the same boat as I, working out their own issues. It eased a lot my very difficult sense of having been so badly marginalised in this country, as though there was something particularly wrong with me, which I did not believe in.

The SDN workshop was a very nurturing environment, which I needed so badly in Australia, since I missed badly my warm family. About 18 adult participants sat in a circle and we started by introducing ourselves, where we were in our lives, and what we expected from this residential. Then we negotiated the so-called SDN contract. It was aimed at providing equal opportunity to all to be heard if we had something to contribute, and to practice mutual respect by accepting each other as we were, rather than being judgmental. After having been severely criticised in marriage, such SDN format was very healing to me and gave a tremendous boost to my self-esteem, badly

13   Schumacher was the author of *Small is Beautiful*, and paying attention to grass-roots level, privately and as a community.

shattered by my disastrous beginnings in Australia. I needed people who would have a similar, holistic approach to human mental, emotional, behavioural and social issues, and was delighted to have found in SDN exactly that – a group of friendly, open minded, intelligent and educated people, like me, who were into personal healing, growth and social development, as complementary one to another. I was also very happy that there was experiential education at SDN, rather than any authoritarian preaching or teaching that I always had an issue with.

My children did not enjoy the first SDN residential, but were bored by themselves, waiting for us adults to finish our workshops. So they refused to attend again. SDN did not have any particular system to provide for children – they had to find their own way. While I wanted my own time at the residential, as a sole parent, I had a bit of a problem with that. Having learned a lot from my children, I now think, as I didn't then, that it could have been a good challenge for SDN to find a way to integrate children as full members of our society, into our process.

A couple of years later, other members' children who were present at that residential, took their own initiative in that sense, at the very end. We used to put up the final show, which was great fun and a joyful community building time. These kids choose to take part in it, and gave us serious adult members, the most insightful, tremendously creative and extremely humorous, incisive feedback, by acting out a hilarious satire about adult SDN-ers. To me it was the most worthwhile and funniest part of the show that I probably enjoyed more than anything else in SDN.

Reflecting on the contract and process

What principles are embedded in the contract that you found important?

The central concept in SDN contract of not judging each other was completely new to me. Brought up to be a proud, judgmental intellectual, I became very arrogant too. But since my ex-husband pointed out to me, a couple of years before coming to Australia, that when I found people stupid, that's where my learning was, I realized how my arrogance was very self-limiting and, in fact, stupid itself. I wanted to change it, but did not know how. The SDN contract showed me, for the very first time in my life, that respect for each other, just as we are, was the way, rather than top priority being to win an argument and control each other. My marriage had suffered a lot from that, so mutual respect for each other's boundaries, as stated in the contract, that 'we accept each other as we find each other', was deeply healing to me.

I was also greatly relieved by realising that other intellectual participants must have had the same issue as I and felt the need to correct it – otherwise we wouldn't have spent so much time setting up the rules for not being judgmental! I appreciated very much that dealing with our own judgment was the corner stone for a new, mutually healing, instead of conflict based community.

I also valued a lot that all workshops were to be experiential. I had already experienced such workshops at Bredbo Confest, and found out that experiential education could be, and was life changing for me. But Confest workshops were pre-conceived by facilitators. By contrast, in SDN, for the very first time I participated actively with everyone else in a truly democratic, grass root process of creating and organizing the whole of the agenda. It was a relief to my soul, badly hurt by authoritarian limitations in my personal and professional life.

Putting the principles of our contract in practice was sometimes challenging. For example, one presenter once lectured at us and spoke on behalf of all of us, "We all think..." I objected to such authoritarian trespassing of our boundaries, and asked him to talk for himself. He continued in the same vein, and I became really angry, because other participants kept silent, except for one other person. SDN did not have anything in place to deal with such blatant breachs of our contract, except the agreed-upon principle of cooperative inquiry in an experiential way. Therefore I did not attend any more SDN workshops.

I also felt uncomfortable in workshops when Joan Iceton would repeatedly admonish Ned quite angrily, "Get into your adult, Ned!" whenever he was joyful, or emotional, or funny. To me, the value of the SDN members' contract and of our workshops was above all in being allowed to own and express in the safe and therefore healing environment our own inner child, and certainly not to be told off for doing just that, from an authoritarian 'adult' point of view. On those occasions I would therefore say to Ned something like, "We love you as you are, Ned!" Nobody else ever said anything, which I was disappointed with.

I had to work out on my own about what to do. Eventually I forced myself to approach Joan, asking her with genuine interest, instead of avoiding her as up till then, how did she feel in our workshops. She appeared to me for the very first time to be relieved, and even happy to look me in the eye, as she said emphatically, "It is an agony for me!" I found it very sad, especially seeing Ned's enthusiasm about SDN, and I felt compassionate towards her.

But how come her agony was not attended to? How come she, who was always there, did not attend to it in our workshops, but kept trying to control Ned? It confirmed my sense that deeper personal emotional realities needed to be dealt with more appropriately. SDN was conceived as a socially healing environment, yet in practice it was still not enough, even though in most workshops we were working on that. When I was saying, "In order to be socially effective as we want to be, we have to attend to our own deeper issues", it was understood and agreed upon mentally, but it was not upheld when it came to such personal conflict. Such silently ignored conflict, that stayed unresolved as though at the centre of SDN 'family', reinforced my life-long attitude to attend in a healing way to every emotional bit that other people didn't want to look at.

On the other hand, SDN gatherings that I attended (three annual and two weekend workshops) provided me with some good tools for resolving conflict, like active listening, as alternative to painful, arrogant arguing and interrupting each other.

In SDN there were two formats – workshops and presentations. Workshops were for personal growth and development, fun, healing and sharing. I resonated strongly with that, because it was what I needed at that stage of my life. Presentations were about some member's professional and community projects. I appreciated that, and could understand that presenters were keen on being heard by likeminded people in SDN, and get some constructive feedback. But I did not have a workplace, or community. Instead, I had too much on my private plate, so I was not attracted to the presentation format. I would spend time with my children instead, which was what we needed. I appreciated that SDN members accepted that too, even though we had the contract rule that we would all attend all group work.

I was very impressed by and most grateful for the principle and practice that Ned would sum up all distances and/or moneys that each member had to travel and pay transport for, to get from our respective home town to the residential, and then he would divide the sum(s) by the number of participants, and those who lived closer to the venue contributed what was considered to be their fair share of overall travel price, which was then reimbursed to those who had to travel longer distance, like me. It was the most practical, financially egalitarian, collectively as much as mutually supportive principle and practice that I ever came across, including up till now. Having been brought up on the basis of the communist idea: "To everyone according to their needs, from everyone as much as they can." and having wracked my brains in my teenage years to think how it could work, I thought that it was too idealistic to ever be applicable, due to greedy and lazy members in any group. That did not exist in SDN, so it was implemented smoothly and I appreciated it very much.

Overall, I was very happy with SDN, and thought that many more people could benefit from knowing about it and joining in. I suggested more active recruiting for new members, but there was a resistance to it by most 'old hands'. The rationale was that numbers for workshops needed to stay limited, while I thought that we could have more workshops, in more locations. I found that resistance self-limiting and stifling a mentality, not really congruent with SDN mission – to contribute as much as we could to developing the healthier society.

An odd bird: cultural differences

While it was good to be heard in SDN, it was not my top priority since I come from a very outspoken and interactive Serbian culture and family background, in which I was normally very well heard. I wanted more complete communication loop, about emotional issues especially, and it was not happening enough for me in SDN.

While we shared and actively listened to each other in groups, and expressed our state verbally or by drawing, live sculpting or otherwise, there was no commentary – there was no, really, enough ongoing complete feedback for my liking. I understood it as an Anglo Saxon dominant cultural trait, definitely unlike Serbian culture, which is much more emotionally aware and freely expressive. I was possibly the only odd bird from ethnic point of view, with somewhat different cultural needs. Probably nobody was aware of it, since I did not bring it up either, because it appeared that being more emotionally transparent was culturally embarrassing to most participants.

Emotional feedback and the intellectual agenda

*I thought an important part of the workshops was getting feedback –
people wanted it and many people did feel they got it. So what do you
mean by feedback?*

Thoughtful feedback was the usual thing in the presentation format.
But it's different from what I'm talking about – the emotional response
from the depth of one's gut. In our workshop format, or even in small
groups which were allowing for more intimate sharing, we just listened and that was it. I appreciated it was respectful, but there was no
complete feed forward-feedback communication loop, that is, from
my point of view, essential to deeper human relating.

*And is that when you felt you needed to spend much more time on the
personal, emotional?*

Yes, definitely. One of the reasons that I decided not to attend SDN
workshops any more was that it was very much intellectual, while the
more emotional transparency and connection was, in my experience,
taking place in personal friendships, not so much in workshops.

And did that smother the emotional?

Yes, that's how I felt, for instance when Joan's bottled up emotions
and judgment would be projected onto Ned. Everyone other than me
would just ignore it and keep silent. While the tension in the room
would become so palpable, people did not attend to their own emotions openly, nor supported Ned or Joan to do anything about theirs,
probably because nobody knew otherwise. But I felt quite aggravated
by that. I needed more attention to healing work on emotional aspects
of our group experience in relation to such repetitive blatant breach of
our contract. I needed to face all difficult emotions openly, and resolve
them urgently and appropriately, instead of sitting on them as time
bombs.

While I appreciated learning about mutually affirming, positive
feedback, which was a rule in SDN, that same rule, without additional tools to deal with occasional conflict and resulting emotions,
resulted in powerless collective denial. My emotional intelligence was
telling me in no uncertain terms that we needed a more appropriate
group response. In retrospect, I think that it would have been helpful
to have been encouraged (as in recovery circles), to own all our feelings and say honestly, "This is how I feel now," irrespective of what

our emotional response might have been, and/or to ask (as in coaching) Joan, "How is it a problem for you that Ned is not all the time in his adult?" That way the obvious conflict and related difficult feelings between some members would have been more appropriately attended to and hopefully healed in a win-win manner.

To deal more effectively with my own and other people's deeper emotions, I opted out of SDN, focused on self-healing and became a healer and qualified therapist. I am grateful that SDN provided me with significant initial support and some valuable tools on my healing path. Later I have been working as a social developer in my way, by running my own healing circle in Sydney in late 1990s, and by working one to one, especially on deeply suppressed emotional and spiritual issues. My work indicates that denial of our dark side, individually and/or collectively, is the very root cause of any relationship, group, social and environmental problems, and that healing such denial heals practically all issues and conditions, including e.g. cancer and gangrene. I see the popular New Age, and SDN option for positive feedback only as unsustainable – a latest variation of an age-old cultural addition to 'positives', e.g. riches, that manifests as greed. In all natural sustainable processes positive and negative are inseparable, as in a bio-feedback loop that provides balance to all life-sustaining processes. With positive bio-feedback only, we would keep breathing in without ever breathing out, or keep eating, or walking, or sleeping endlessly. Likewise, I find that emotional and spiritual suppression, in the name of anything positive (peace, good relationship, etc.) is an individual and social systemic dysfunction, resulting in unsustainable compensation systems (consumerism, compulsive and addictive behaviours, and so called terminal or incurable conditions), and environmental destruction. Since SDN's objective is personal and social development towards sustainability, I consider that attending appropriately to all group engendered conflict and resulting emotions is essential.

Appreciating Ned

As the person who invited me to join SDN, Ned was a very important figure in my life in the late 1980s, when I needed so much healing from my midlife crisis, and recovery from having been so deeply disenchanted with society at large. Back then, I did not review my whole

SDN experience with anybody, only personally thanked Ned each time. I appreciated that he was open-minded about me not attending SDN workshops for my personal reasons, yet he kept in touch with me.

I appreciated Ned tremendously for having had the honesty and courage to step out of his comfortable social status, position and income as MD, to co-found the SDN, and to keep working through it according to his conviction, as well as for having set up the NED.

I also value Ned's initiative to have this book compiled, in order to provide a more wholesome perspective on SDN and its members, and I am looking forward to reading it. I think that complete feedback is sadly missing in our society, which contributes to various dysfunctions, and that a fair reflection from all contributors, including Ned, is going to clarify many things on SDN, that might benefit from it in its own growth.

Chapter 9

Change and continuity
across three decades

David Purnell and Chris Larkin

Introducing David

I've been in Canberra for most of my life – worked in the Public Service and in the university administration at ANU[14], and I've also worked on peace education and conflict resolution as a mediator and working with the Quakers. So I've done a whole mixture of things.

I came into contact with Ned some time before I knew anything about SDN, because Ned was doing a continuing education seminar at ANU, which in those days was looking at a much broader idea of continuing education and how people might see the future. I went along and was impressed by his presentation – his broad approach to things and the issues of social change and in particular personal change. In those days such things weren't talked about as often. That was in the 70s. Ned seemed to fit into that whole way of looking at things that I was interested in, saying, 'How can we bring people together so that we can look at the way forward in a constructive way?' So it was a good introduction. And then I discovered through him that SDN existed. But it took me a few more years to actually go to a workshop.

Introducing Chris

Well I qualified as a Social Worker when I was 21 year-old and have been working as one for most of the time since then, primarily for ACT Health and Community Health. I've lived in Canberra a long time, two kids, but grew up in Camden.

As a social work student back in my uni days, '69, or my young social work days in the early 70s, I saw an article in the *Journal of Social Issues* where Ned had written about working with people in rural communities. And I remember being quite excited about it. But I didn't know him then.

I saw myself as a radical social worker and I was working with Parent Support Services here in Canberra – in the late 70s. It had a kind of community development approach. Barbara Hicks was involved with that as a social worker consultant and she was the first one who told me about this network. I think it was probably '82 – the first SDN workshop I went to.

Early SDN

David: I think SDN was started in 1975 by John and Ned. I think I went to my first one in 1984.

Chris: David and I went up together – it started our romance!

David: I'd always had a strong interest in change. I'd been connected with an organisation called Australian Frontier and it was a pioneering group set up through the church networks, looking at the whole issue of responsibility for things. They'd draw together people from different disciplines and ask, 'What is the responsibility of this community towards the aged, or town planning or whatever it was'. They would meet over a couple of days. Having been involved in those kinds of meetings, I was then attracted particularly to what Ned was doing in terms of getting people together and looking at issues.

Chris: What appealed to me in those early days was that it was leading-edge knowledge – things that we might not have heard much about otherwise. Barbara was a very stimulating enabler of people and she ran workshops on transactional analysis, gestalt, Steiner and so on. SDN was all part of looking at things in that more interesting and dynamic way – looking at our personal stuff while being interested in the bigger picture and how it connected.

In the late 80s I was involved in quite a lot of group work. And part of that was influenced by my training and professional base – but part of it would have been influenced by SDN and the experiences of it. Because, in some ways, I wouldn't have had the opportunity for these experiences otherwise. So it encouraged me to have models of processes that I could introduce, that might not otherwise have happened. That was quite a strong principle – that you've got to try it on yourself before you try it on someone else. And that was undermining that type of professionalism that was around at that time – where you had to be the expert and the others are the learners. So in some ways it gave me the courage and the skills – modelling.

And also, people came from different backgrounds who I wouldn't normally have come across, people who were really intelligent, turned-on, concerned people in their local communities but who hadn't necessarily got a professional background. So it was a good way to connect with a cross section of people.

But there hasn't been a lot of ethnic, cross-cultural stuff. It was good when Tiyana came – a different influence[15]. But there wasn't a lot of that. So in some ways it was quite monocultural, but in other ways it wasn't at all.

The workshops

David: The workshops always start with an open slate and people will throw up ideas and then the program gets developed. The Contract is agreed to at the beginning of each workshop – about people taking responsibility for their own stuff. So there has always been an agreement about things.

Chris: It was a fun process. You never knew what there'd be on the agenda.

David: In the workshop situation it's John who reacts to what people are doing. He's a more spontaneous person and responds to things in the moment, what's happening. He and Ned challenge each other in different ways and that's good. They're complementary

Chris: Ned is more an ideas person and I think an ideas person is more likely to get the kudos than a process person.

SDN and the workshops were about social justice, and that we have to work at the personal level at the same time.

15   See chapter 8.

I've heard that early on there was some tension between those who wanted to deal with the macro and others with the micro issues.

David: I think my interest initially was with the macro side of it – looking at the structures of society and where we're going. But also having done some work with Life Line on personal growth, it didn't surprise me when the two things came together in the workshops. But it meant the workshops were quite challenging and difficult at times. At least in those earlier years we certainly didn't look upon them as a rest!

There were a number of people who were more interested in the macro. But there were others who brought the more personal, micro, stuff in; people being confronted about what they'd said or how they felt about something – some interaction taking place. I think there is a bit of self-selection – that has to be an inevitable thing. And I think there were some people that decided that it wasn't for them and so they dropped out. All along there have been some people who turned up for one workshop and never turned up again because it just didn't quite mesh with the way they were feeling. Maybe they were confronted in a way they didn't expect or like. Most of the people there were fairly assertive.

There were people like Beth and Mary and Joan McCarthy who were prepared to use different methods like drawing or dance, meditation – some different modes. And so that provided a nice mixture of processes.

Chris: Using these approaches was really good for me. And there's not so much of that now.

Were people comfortable with that?

David: I think once people were there, they accepted that it was part of the deal and if someone wanted to run something like that, they had responsibility for running that session in the way they wanted to run it. And that was understood. So I think that even if you felt slightly uncomfortable about it, you went along with it. And you probably learned something as a result. You could opt out, but that didn't happen very much.

Chris: Well I've got a different take on that, because I think that's something that evolved. In the early days it was tougher and you were expected to be at all of the sessions. But people voted with their feet. Like I remember that time at Guthega where Barbara just went off and then Beth went for a walk. I remember that in the early days John

Russell was very strict about it. He'd say, 'We're here and we're all participants and we've all got to know what's going on'. And with my group-work background I think I agreed with that in principle. But we're much more laid back now. I think Aboriginal people's culture of responding to what's happening now, rather than being ruled by time frames, has influenced us. The earlier workshops were probably more personally challenging. We were doing the Esalen kind of thing in the 80s – getting really confronted[16].

David: The workshop was basically a safe environment in which to do that. But it took a bit of time to get used to the different ways people would react to things. And sometimes things would go off the rails and you'd have to try and regroup and have a bit of debriefing on what had happened and why. So it was quite a volatile thing in some situations.

So what sort of things kept it together then?

Chris: Well I think it was because you're working so closely together with people – people who were prepared to be open, and somewhat of risk takers to be there in the first place. So you don't have particularly conservative personalities. That's a good start. It was about the processes of sharing and going through that together.

Those early workshops were a real high for me. For example I remember the happiness of us all walking crazily in a conga line to the music of Pachelbel's Canon. We were quite creative in those days.

We had my kids and a couple of other kids up in Armidale in 1987. It was part of a holiday. They didn't want to be part of the sessions all the time, of course, so they entertained themselves in our vicinity. They decided to do this play for us. I think they were the ones who came up with the idea of mimicking us, so it was a wonderful surprise. What I liked about them being there was that it gave them good role models of adults.

16   The Esalen Institute was founded in California in 1962. Its alternative educational approach included experiential workshops blending East/West philosophies and practices.

Themes across the decades

As we talk it seems that there were a number of different themes that came up in each decade. It's a really interesting historical path.

Chris: It would have been good to have minutes that talked about the topics that were covered. There's not much around. One of the issues in the 80s was gender. That was a big one for me. I saw myself as a feminist and I remember challenging guys about their language, or taking too much air time – some more than others. Ned was good to challenge on that, and a few others.

And did you feel that could be worked through?

Chris: I think it was allowable in that context and that was part of the good thing of it – because in other contexts you didn't have that opportunity to explore that. But I felt safe to say, in that situation, 'Well look here – this is what I'm seeing happening'. And I'm not aware of any great rifts that happened. People might have got pissed off with each other, but we did it – safely – yeah. But Ned is probably, of that core group, the one I got most annoyed with. But I've softened as I've got older, as we do. And he has become less dominating as he's got older. And he was open to people telling him that.

David: The workshops used to be much longer – six or seven days – so there was more time anyway.

So what key themes do you see: both similarities and things that have evolved?

David: In terms of themes – issues related to feminism and gender in general. People like me were involved in the men's movement, and some of that came through in our workshops, and in social justice in general in the earlier times. Nowadays you tend to get more specific stuff about restorative justice, for example. In the 90s we talked about war and peace. Ned's always been into social change and where we're headed and the way society is going – his analysis of political events, international trends – that always has quite an impact on the workshops.

Chris: Yeah – the big macro-economic picture and I appreciated that. Ben was also very theoretical and interested in macro issues – always.

David: And that's when some of the indigenous justice issues came through – in the '90s – with people like Beth who was quite active.

And several times Ned managed to get some Indigenous people to come to a couple of the workshops in Armidale: Ray Kelly was one, and a woman who was running an Aboriginal school in Armidale.

Chris: Back in the '80s Kath Wray was very interested in a technique relating to past lives. There was quite some interest in psychic stuff, and there was a bit of a division on that because some thought it was a load of rubbish. It was something that interested me. Kath did a session once where she got us to do past lives regressions – so quite an intense process. That would have been the time when people didn't opt out. So there was that trusting thing of, 'OK, if someone brings it, we'll do it'. We had rituals around the seasons; do you remember? In the late '80s in Jindabyne I remember we walked up to the oval – we had candles – probably Beth's idea. I like the variety. One of the current conversations is about the internet.

Local workshops

David: I find it quite difficult to judge what appeals to people. We've had much more difficulty running local workshops. We've tried different formats; for example of having an evening for people to get to know what SDN's about. Earlier on we had a few workshops at Congo, on the South Coast of New South Wales, for people from Canberra, and these were well received by those who were there. They have local workshops in Victoria with varying success. And they did one in Deniliquin – which was a bit different as it focused on a particular group of people. But it's hard to know what the best way to get people in is. We've found it quite difficult, here, to get new people to come and stick around.

Going, and not going

You have to make quite a commitment to go, don't you?

David: I've gone fairly regularly to the national workshops – probably every second year.

What kept you going?

For me it was quite unusual. That's because the sorts of things I was involved in were mainly about taking responsibility for issues or activities, whether in Quakers or at work. And so to have the time of a few days when I didn't have any of that responsibility – and it was just an opportunity to reflect and be with other interesting and stimulating people – to me it was a refreshment. So I took it as a nice part of a break. And even though I didn't get to every single one, I really enjoyed the ones I did go to. So that's kept me going for a long period.

Chris: The main reasons that I haven't been involved in recent years, until 2008 again, is because of other priorities. I decided, after a while, in the '90s, that I'd rather just have time off to be on holiday than go to an SDN workshop as I'm still in paid employment. Whereas in the earlier days it was more important for me to have that input. And that's because I wasn't getting it anywhere else.

And what was that?

Well, the chance to explore – as peers but not in your work context – the personal and the political. And it was fun. For me it's fun to be challenged.

Hmm, so why didn't I want to do it in the 90s? Well, maybe, I just got to a position where it wasn't so challenging any more, having done it for a while. It's not so interesting if you've done it four or five times, I suppose.

A community

David: For me SDN was fairly seamless because it was connected with all the other things I was involved with, like the conflict resolution work, the stuff with the men's movement and all those things. But with SDN it was an independent network with which to check base, get a bit of feedback, and get some stimulating thoughts about directions you could take things.

Chris: Do you remember when you'd been asked to go into politics and you'd explored that at a session? So it was also used for people to think about their life direction.

David: That still goes on – people weighing up options. There are usually half oldies, half newies –about 20 people (18 this time, 2008). And there is still a strong group mentality and that's a good feeling.

Chris: It means we're part of a community.

Chapter 10

Being Listened To

Jean Leeman

Introducing Jean

I found my way into the Social Developers' Network through my partner Ben. I'm a social worker of 35 plus years' experience. Within that, I've always been aware of community development. It was an integral part of our training which covered individual counselling, group work, community development and social action, though when I trained in the sixties the emphasis was on one to one or family counselling. I've mainly worked with individuals – mainly in child and family work both here and in the UK, and in migrant work. Now, in my current work – within the church, with abuse of power issues. I use community development as well as undertaking individual and group work.

And it wasn't until meeting Ben, and him being a very close friend of John Russell, that I began to be aware of SDN. That was in the 70s. So I knew about it fairly early on.

I was aware that John would come to these workshops (and that he wanted his family to come). It was a little while before Ben came. Then it was many more years before I joined. I must have been to at least nine workshops, mostly consecutively – I've been in Melbourne, Armidale, and Guthega. I also went to (and helped organize) the Victorian regional workshops except one when I had to work.

Emotional support

What were the driving forces for getting to a workshop, or not coming?

Sometimes there were practical issues for not coming. Perhaps Ben was away and I didn't come by myself, probably because they could be very challenging. There have been times in our workshops where they've been fairly confronting and fiery and have taken a lot of emotional energy. So doing that without feeling emotionally supported (it's interesting that I saw Ben more as the support in the early days rather than the whole group). I think now I'd be happy to come on my own because I feel people are really really supportive.

Support, conflict, challenge and engagement

How have those challenging issues been handled?

As an SDN member we are left with our own responsibility to either raise issues with people or to not let them impact on the sessions. So I've had to learn to raise them, and have discussions about what I've felt and how I've responded to what others said. And that can be a challenge.

But it can also be a challenge when you are talking about your own work or issue. And you've got people looking at it from an entirely different perspective. That's a good challenge but it can be an uncomfortable one. There have been times when people haven't necessarily felt supported, because some people tell others what they should do – and are resented. They can give you options and ideas, but never tell you what to do.

There have been times when the women have spoken up as a group, by saying 'that's just a man's way of thinking about it and there are other perspectives'. At times we've done role plays and small groups and that's been powerful. Gender – it just pops up from time to time. Strong women characters do balance things with the strong male characters.

This workshop hasn't raised gender in the same ways, just as it hasn't raised race issues. There was one workshop where race issues were raised by an Indigenous man struggling to engage with the group, but also talking about how things were from his perspective. That raised cultural issues. It was one of those workshops where we couldn't bond enough – and issues weren't resolved.

But there is always a value in what happens over these days. Sometimes you wished it hadn't happened, but on the whole it's really been a great benefit. It's a way to recharge and get on with what you are doing. I see this as a private thing, that I'm coming for my own purposes, although I know it does benefit my work and so the community too. At times I've been so pleased that Ben could share and get assistance with an issue – it's been important as a couple coming to these workshops.

The importance of building community

Has there been a shift in the way the group works together?

Yes. I think there have been times when the community hasn't stayed together as well. I always found the Guthega ones great, because of the intensity of being up in the mountains and where people couldn't come and go. That was the opportunity to really work things through. The ones I found most difficult were centrally in Armidale when a number of different people came and went. I think that broke the sense of community and therefore the trust probably wasn't as great. So perhaps some of the issues that came up couldn't be resolved in the same way.

So has it been a spatial, place aspect rather than an evolution over time?

No, not altogether – because it's been very good at times. And of course it's a personal perspective where it was good for me at one time and not so good at another. I think it depends on each workshop. The basic principles are there, and it's when we don't adhere to those basic principles, that we get into strife. And it depends on the people, where they are at and what they bring to each one. But I think that being an enforced community has its advantages for this sort of work.

I keep on trying to think what's different about this workshop (Uralla 2006); that it's so super every day and that people, so early on in the workshops, could have a session like last night of being able to challenge and raise issues but with less emotional intensity that hasn't led to tears. And I think it's been positive this time, because sometimes the tears have also be really positive, but this feels like people haven't got so distressed – they haven't needed to get so distressed. People have expressed emotion but more on a level that's working through. But maybe we haven't got to the depths yet! And that's always possible!

A mix of people

There have been so many different people over the years – creative people. To me one of the most important things about coming, and that has encouraged me to come, has been the mix of people – their wide experience, their commitment to change, and to improving things in the world for people.

I think it's changed from time to time. We organized Victorian ones (John Russell, Rosaria Palmesi, Ben and I) – a different flavour, but perhaps there's a broader perspective at the national one. People like Kath Wray stand out to me in terms of the tremendous courage, enthusiasm, commitment, and the way she engaged us with what she'd been doing and perhaps ways that we'd been able to help her in terms of moving on with what she was doing. One lady was in organic farming and I wouldn't have met her without the national SDN.

Ned

Ned's always been essential to SDN through his contacts – his keeping in touch – his networking over the year in between. That keeps up the momentum, keeps it going, brings new issues, new possibilities, and new people coming in. So I see Ned's role as crucial. His theoretical understanding and his experience in community development has been a major factor in the SDN. There's times when it's perhaps been his baby and maybe people rely on him too much. But there have been attempts over the time – and I think that has changed – that perhaps he was more in charge and domineering in earlier times. He's learnt, and people have challenged him to stand back and be a participant in the group – and that's been healthy for the group.

Ned's a person who takes a lot of interest in other people, which I really appreciate. He is also a person who has some of his fixed ideas which I don't appreciate in Ned. Ned is someone who I have a sense of him wanting or expecting more of me and I think over the years he's learnt to let me be and do my thing. Ned's always been someone who would be very prominent, sometimes dominant. There have been times when I've had issues with Ned's dominance.

Ned likes to look at the macro very often, and there've been a number, usually male, who have focused in on the macro issues – Ben being one of them. And there are others who want to look at the micro, personal issues and how we might change ourselves – which is what Ned is on about too – as people, to be able to go out and do the work we do. Ned can do both, and he does that in his own daily life. And I think that's admirable to see someone living out what they are talking about.

Ned has a huge amount of integrity as a person. Sometimes Little Ned is the one who needs others to support him, while at other times he's the teacher and leader – it's complex and it's good. Ned can be very warm to you, although at other times he puts a distance. I think within SDN he's gained another group of people who he can relate very closely to and that helps bring him back from that aloofness.

The space to be heard

The other thing that I really appreciate about SDN is that the creative listening is really powerful. When we do it well within a session – when someone is presenting and seeking assistance in working their way through whatever their issue is – it is really powerfully supportive. Sometimes it's confronting, but it gives you the space to be heard and it's the power in being heard that I've found so freeing and supportive.

Is that partly because you wouldn't find that somewhere else?

I could find that somewhere else, so I'm not sure what is different about that. I'd do that individually in my supervision – I've had good supervisors. But it's the power of sitting down with a group of people who all focus in and support and listen and give feedback. That's what's different about SDN and I don't think that happens anywhere else. It's the group – it's the community that's created that's so unique in this. And people will follow up afterwards, or you can follow up with people afterwards. You can do that to a certain extent after a professional workshop, but this is a living community.

It's important to get across the essence of how people become a community in SDN, from this very very loose community of connections, for the period of time we are together. That takes a lot of energy and effort – but has positive outcomes. I'd like it to be seen that SDN is not as an exclusive group, where people can't come in and out of, but that people are welcome to come at the time that suits them. And that they don't owe it to SDN to just come for the sake of coming – but that they come because they are really committed to what's going on.

I'd like people to know what the benefits are of SDN and the creative and liberating outcomes for people, and seeing how those people operate. For example we've seen David Crew come for the first time, having operated without that sort of support around him, for a number of years and done a fantastic job, but having come to a stage where he needs something else. And this is the sort of group, hopefully, that can give him that sort of input.

Chapter 11

Making a Difference

Mary Porter

Introductions

I'm British by birth, arriving in Australia at the age of 12 in 1954 with my parents and 3-year-old sister. I came from a working class background and as a child I soon developed a strong service ethic, courtesy of my parents. At a very young age I became a British Red Cross volunteer and on leaving formal education quickly undertook training as a general nurse and midwife.

From the mid 60's I moved to the Top End of the Northern Territory with my then husband, serving as a remote area registered nurse, living and working in remote indigenous communities, for 10 years off and on. I worked voluntarily, as was the expectation of the 'wife' apart from the last 3 years, when we were stationed at Dhupuma, residential college for indigenous students. I was known as 'sister in charge', a grand title for the only medical staff there!

When the oldest of our three children turned twelve my then husband and I needed to return south to provide more appropriate education for him. He had experienced a deal of disruption to his education due to a childhood disability. As we were Commonwealth public servants by then, we transferred to Canberra.

This changed my life's direction. Canberra felt like a foreign country, however my mother advised me to 'get out there and talk to people'.

I soon found myself on a steering committee to help set up a regional community service in the burgeoning area of Canberra known as "nappy valley", Tuggeranong. Unable to return to paid work, with small children and no car, I became a volunteer for the organisation and when funds became available, the service appointed me as its first part-time employee. This organisation is now a multimillion concern, providing a wide variety of community services.

A brief stint working for a Federal Minister, another volunteer position, working to set up a peak body for volunteers in the ACT, led to me becoming its first CEO. After twelve years at the helm, experiencing domestic violence in my first marriage, a divorce and re-marriage, I was becoming frustrated at the response of the ACT Government to issues in relation to the not for profit sector.

Feeling stale in my CEO role and contemplating retirement in my early 60's, my now husband (political junky) said "you have been asked before to run for the ACT Legislative Assembly, get in there and make a difference". My parents had been staunch members of the British Labour and I was a member of the ALP, I decided to follow my father's example – he stood for local council back in Surrey when I was a child. I was first elected to the ACT Legislative Assembly in October of 2004.

How did you meet Ned?

Early in my time as a community development worker, in the mid-1980s, a flyer came across my desk from a David Purnell, inviting me to a meeting for people interested in social development. This sparked my interest and curiosity. At the meeting people related their recent experience at a Social Developers' Network workshop held over a few days at Jindabyne. This I found *very* interesting.

What sparked your interest?

People described a process of participants coming together in a live-in workshop situation to talk about whatever issues and topics they particularly wanted to discuss. There was no set agenda, no preconceived outcome, a place to contribute, learn from others and share. Each person coming from the place in their lives at the moment. From a small child I was taught that one's purpose in life was to make a difference. At the time I was enthused by a mission to change the world, at least my bit of it. I hadn't met Ned then, however, I soon learnt that this was his mission too, but on a grander scale.

What were your early workshop experiences?

A years later I signed up for a workshop in Jindabyne. After I made this decision, and as I was on my way there, I suddenly thought 'maybe this isn't a good idea!' I was very nervous on arrival (I would think this is not an uncommon reaction by first timers – what am I in for?)

Are you able to describe the process?

I became interested because I heard someone else describe their experience, what they had gained. Once there I found myself sharing a room with a woman I had just met, facing the prospect of at least four days with mostly strangers, 24 hours a day, sharing domestic tasks, cooking, cleaning and, at the same time engaging in thought-provoking, often challenging, group discussion. I can't describe it any other way – it's the total experience. What I believe is crucial is the support you give each other and the quiet reflection that also occurs.

I later attended workshops that were catered for, but I believe something is missing when that happens. Each workshop is different as each is a different group of people, with different contributions to make, different issues. At first I found Ned's presence dominated the direction of discussion, he appeared to be more comfortable if the discussion focused on the big picture, or macro issues, and not the micro. Some women in particular would prefer to introduce the micro and also the more creative and contemplative ways of working and exploring topics.

I found this dichotomy fascinating. When talking one to one with Ned, a different Ned emerges for me, a deeply sensitive and caring person who was very aware of the inner self. I remember the phrase that he would use – 'big Ned and little Ned'. His wife Joan was a very interesting woman, a quiet, strong influence in the group, sitting knitting, like our mother, while Ned appeared to be the father figure. I believe Joan's early death from cancer affected Ned deeply, as you would expect.

Many of us find it hard to describe the SDN process, I believe this is due to the fact that each of us has our own perception of what it is and what it means. I never feel that I have explained SDN adequately to someone who asks. Some may ask if this network and the workshops have some kind of religious or new world pop-psychology overtones, far from it. People who are part of the network, and attend workshops from time to time, may have a religious or spiritual belief that motivates or drives them, others may be agnostic, atheist, humanist or are passionate about a certain cause, such as our fragile environment. Others may describe what they do as social entrepreneurship, or social development, hence the name of the network.

Group dynamics: change, growth and remaking.

How did the workshops change?

At first I perceived there were some taboo subjects, like sexuality, gender politics, examples of the micro. There were sometimes clashes of ideas and opinions, not unexpected or unhealthy. Some of the women, and men as well, would raise these micro topics for discussion and others would prefer to focus more on global politics, fixing the ills of the world.

It's interesting you talk about the division between macro and micro, because one of the things that I see as unique about the Social Developers' Network – it seemed to be about the individual and getting out into the social world, but it sounds like it took some time for that to be evident.

There appeared to be a belief amongst some that discussing our experiences of the public world, rather than our personal world, was more important. However, it is often through discussing the way each of us worked through our personal challenges and the realities for each of us, that in that process we would become stronger, refreshed. Perhaps I sensed an unwritten rule, one didn't, for example, talk about how attending a SDN workshop had helped one with a serious domestic situation, perhaps a difficult relationship with a significant person. This seemed to change when a long-term SDN member trusted the group process enough to share very personal issues about his relationships. There was a definite shift then as far as I recall.

It is probably true that gender made a difference in the way we approached the workshops. Another occasion I recall, when there was another definite shift, was when the group participated in a clown workshop session. Those who aren't familiar with the process might understand it best by recalling that, as a child, one can dress up as another character, without giving much thought as to why you chose to become that other person. I became a fairy floss fairy, born at a fair in a fairy floss machine! Another very straight methodical man took on the persona of a woman. Ned dressed in a chenille dressing gown and cloth hat, becoming an older woman and found himself crying, I suspect for the world he so desperately wanted to save from itself. I think that workshop taught us we can't be totally serious about fixing the world's ills – we need to laugh and cry together sometimes.

The workshops have evolved through added creativity, more reflection, small group work, as well as the larger group sessions, and a relaxation of the rule that everyone should be at every session) although attending the whole workshop is still seen as important, not just popping in for a day or two). The live-in principle is also relaxed now (for example, people can stay at accommodation nearby).

Fun and relaxation has always been part of the SDN experience and there is time to visit a local attraction such as a rain forest walk, a nearby gorge, or a short bush walk. One feature I really valued was the party on the last night when I and others would love to become creative, writing lyrics for songs and composing poems. On one occasion family groups attended the workshop, with numbers of children. On the last night the children and young people devised a skit, a portrayal of the workshop through a television interview of Ned, with a teenager playing Ned and another standing beside him acting as his interpreter. It was a brilliant piece of theatre and demonstrated great insight by the young people.

I believe a party on the last evening is important, when a group comes together for the first time it goes through the process of forming, then it is able to let the storming happen, then perform, and finally there is a need to mourn.

Everybody will experience a workshop in their own way, as we all bring our separate life experiences, set of values and expectations. I believe it is necessary to trust the process, with respect, acceptance, and active listening being important tenets. Of course, some may leave a workshop feeling it wasn't for them and may never attend again, however I venture to say not many do.

Have you ever found other avenues that have given you that refreshment, or does SDN offer you something unique?

I haven't found something that takes such a little amount of my time, in terms of the workshop itself, and my involvement which has given me the same opportunity. I could, for instance, join a book club and engage in serious discussion and challenging ideas, however that is quite a regular commitment, whereas SDN allows you to come in and out as you wish and attend a workshop or not as one is able. Each workshop is a unique experience, each group being a new group, each bringing their different issues and topics that the group can explore.

What does that mean for SDN when NED is not around?

Well that is the big question, the unknown. I know Ned desperately wants this and his other endeavours to continue, I think he realises that it will be different, ideally he would love for another 'Ned' to arrive on the scene. It will be a huge responsibility and quite challenging task to continue his life's work, his legacy, after Ned's death.

This it is why it is so good that Ned decided to form an incorporated organisation and select a group of existing network members to work with him as the inaugural board in planning the transition. This has also given Ned the opportunity to see some of this work take shape.

The one thing I hope this book conveys is the humanness of Ned. I want this book to be respectful of him. Our experiences of him are all going to be different, and of the network that he created and nurtured. My experience of him is that he is a very serious man with a serious mission. His life has been a journey of enlightenment, growth and development, as well as pain, letting go of old hurts and facing new challenges. All the time nurturing others, helping us to navigate our own journeys, he is a great nurturer.

How does Ned keep doing that?

Through his music, his daily meditation, his books, extensive reading, travelling, meeting new people, surrounding himself with what appears to be his 'family'. I believe this is how he refreshes himself, in the same way as being involved with the SDN network refreshes me. This is why I am so fortunate to know Ned and be able to share part of his journey.

Post Script - Ned's stamp

I believe that Ned's influence is still very strongly felt. This is normal and is common when a compelling or enigmatic person is largely responsible for an organisation or movement. I have seen that over and over again in my life and observing other organisational processes.

Chapter 12

Perspectives from

Past and Present Participants

Ray Rauscher, Barbara Hicks and David Crew

The final reflections from those involved in SDN come from two early participants who no longer attend workshops but remain within Ned's network, and reflections from a first-time workshop participant. Ray Rauscher and Barbara Hicks responded to Ned's general invitation to contribute to this book, providing written reflections in response to questions from Jo Kijas. David Crew was interviewed by Jo on the final day of his first SDN workshop held in Uralla in January 2006.

Ray Rauscher

What is your background as it relates to Ned and SDN and your interest in social development?

I attended the first series of SD workshops in the early 1970s as a Community Development Officer (CDO) under the Whitlam Area Assistance Plan (AAP). After that I attended a number of SDN workshops and ran some Central Coast SDN workshops in the 1980s.

Back then Ned was an oasis in un-charted territory. I knew little about the self as a social developer. The ability of someone to put social development theory and practice together was immensely attractive. There was equal concern as I, like so many people, stay within our professional roles (my profession was town planning).

To think there was a place for the big picture of society to be explored and to gain tools to act was exciting. It was as if everybody runs around doing bits of social good, but no one puts the 'why' and 'how' of social change together in a single picture.

The scary part was to have to accommodate and deal with the micro aspects of social change, for example people's emotions and hang ups, and one's own. This included: personal development, conflict resolution, and clear listening to all others moving more into a social development framework. Over the ensuring years the acceptance of an agreed contract of workshopping by the SDN participates gave clarity to working cooperatively together.

What are your thoughts on SDN –e.g. what it does, your place in it, what it has meant to you? Tell me about changes over time, what works and what doesn't.

The SDN is a network to support individuals who want to further the aims of social development actions and to ensure they themselves are being effective as initiators of these actions. The SDN is as interested in the individual getting to know himself/herself in being a social activist as SDN is of the actions the person is involved in. Personal growth is thus a priority interest for SDN.

Changes in society since the setting up of the SDN in 1972 has illustrated the clear base SDN had already established in the 1970s. One year's workshop in the early '80s was devoted to creating a SDN manifesto. The document incorporated many of the social inclusiveness interests that abound today. Further, today's interest in sustainable planning for communities fits exactly where SDN has been since the start of its existence.

Tell me about Ned himself; his role in SDN; his theories and philosophies; why and how he's been important to you.

Ned has always been the inspiring and visionary person for SDN. Ned leads by example via involvement in SD activities across the breadth of Australia. He aims to support the person and that person's development in being fully aware of his/her actions in any social actions.

Ned maintains an up-to-date understanding of world social and environmental needs. He gravitates to those organisations that work on the larger picture of needs and actions, as well as the micro needs of communities.

Ned has been important to me for his ability to share ideas and circumstances of social or personal actions. Ned responds with solid suggestions, in an accepting way. He epitomises what SD is all about; a living national treasure.

Barbara Hicks

I met Ned and Joan back in about the early 1970s when I attended my first SDN meeting. I think it was in the Blue Mountains. Later I attended many more in places such as Bowral, before we settled into alternating between the university campus at Armidale and Guthega. Before that, for many years we met annually at the Claude Street Flats in Armidale.

When I first met Joan and Ned it was at the time of Gough Whitlam having gained government and introduced the Australia Plan, I think it was called. There was money available for community development and many people were jumping on the bandwagon. At the time I was employed in Canberra in a Community Health centre setting and doing community development. My background was Social Work.

Ned had done some interesting work with farmers on a Kellogg's scholarship and was employed at UNE. He was trying to find ways to work in the area of social development and still retain his employment in the Adult Education Department of UNE. I think in those early days he ran the SDN workshops as outreach of the UNE Adult Ed program.

There has always been a challenge for those of us in SDN to find the balance between big picture macro stuff and on-the-ground micro stuff. Ned was strong on the macro and would often leave us all confused and bewildered with his big picture monologues, while at the same time he and Joan were very involved in local community initiatives in town and also in their local neighbourhood with the Koori folk.

Ned was always keen for us to present case studies i.e. examples of community development work we were busy with. He provided a format he suggested that we use. This enabled many of us to workshop ideas and projects and possibilities that we were struggling with in our various workplaces. The contrast between big picture (preferred by Ned) and on the ground, or micro picture (Joan's preference), was always a tension in workshops I attended. However, the respect and mutual support of the attendees at SDN gatherings meant that mostly we worked things through.

For myself, a turning point came when I went overseas to study social development at Emerson College in Sussex. This is an international college working with the ideas of Rudolf Steiner. On my return my attendance at SDN annual gatherings became less frequent as my greater commitment was to my Anthroposophical work and a group we had formed called the Institute for Social Development.

While I was at Emerson College Ned and Joan had made some funds available to me that enabled me to continue there when I might otherwise have had to leave. Based on some of my learning, when I returned I refunded that money in due course, hoping it would then be made available for others. I believe Ned has continued to support various members of the Network over the years e.g. by purchasing a computer for one person so they could network with the SDN by email.

Joan died sadly too early in her life after having lived with breast cancer for 10 years, and Ned needed to find a purpose and, I sensed, a use for his estate. So NED (Nurturing Evolutionary Development) was born and a group was formed around Ned that met to help him work out how to establish some sort of foundation that would continue to foster and support social development work.

Within my Anthroposophical Institute for Social Development was a group running workshops, groups, study groups, and for 10 years or more we met every week in North Sydney. This group still meets weekly although I have now moved to Newcastle and can no longer attend. I was unable and no longer interested to commit time and energy into Ned Net or the annual meetings when I had other demands on my time that seemed more local and relevant to my journey.

SDN continues to hold its annual gatherings and I rarely attend. If I do it is more for the social opportunities of meeting up with old friends and to walk the mountains in the Snowy. I know Ned continues to attract new people to these annual gatherings and he travels and keeps in touch with many who have attended over the years.

For me personally there is little or no value in the network any more, except to maintain my friendship with Ned and a few others who have been part of the network for many years – some like me coming in and out. When I do attend it is stimulating and interesting to hear what others are doing. However we have no contact in between the annual meetings and I generally find my local grassroots monthly meetings with my Anthropop colleagues in Newcastle, and others with common interests such as a network of folk interested in bringing about new skills in conflict management in the Hunter, of more value that the yearly meetings.

The issue for me is that there is no common spiritual or even philosophical base from which to launch shared initiatives or endeavours. Each annual meeting is like a conference. And in the course of a year I have many of these to choose from and most offer more than SDN – except the chance to meet up with old and valued colleagues – probably not even friends these days.

Ned himself is a wonderful and generous spirit who has met the challenge of keeping on without his dearly beloved Joan, so remarkably well. He is thoughtful and earnest and courageous and compassionate. He is kind and very hospitable. I have known him for over 30 years and cherish our friendship greatly although these days I rarely see him and so would have to wonder if we still have a friendship. I am sorry we don't see more of each other. I still work and have little opportunity to get to Armidale and it seems Ned does not come to Lake Macquarie. So unless I get to the next SDN annual gathering it will be more years before we meet again.

I have always taken an interest in his gardening endeavours. I have stayed many times in the flat under his lounge room. He is a generous host. Last time I visited him we walked briskly up a nearby hill as part of his exercise regime. I have read many of the books in his library and used to discuss NLP (Neuro Linguistic Programming) endlessly with Joan who was an advanced student.

Over the years Ned has read many books which most of us would not even contemplate. He then tries to summarise and share with us the findings. Often we don't 'get it'. In the past Ned has tried to put his philosophy and ideas into writing and used our annual meetings to test out his theories and philosophies. Many a workshop was spent seeking to understand what Ned was saying and then help him to re-write it in language and concepts the layman might understand.

As noted, all of this is now in the past for me. His importance to me is as a truly earnest and 'good man'. I will always remember him and cherish having known and walked along part of life's path with him and Joan.

David Crew

Interview with Jo Kijas

I turned 44 this year (2006). I live in Wamba Wamba Country with my wife Jeannette (Jenny), who I've been with for 25 years. I grew up in Armidale to academic parents. My father was an adult educationalist. My parents have always been socially aware and engaged. I wanted to become an archaeologist and I was interested in working with Aboriginal communities. But I became very jaded with the academic world because as an archaeologist, I lived this work. I wasn't in and out like many others and I found myself more engaged with the community than other archaeologists were, which created some conflicts. In 2001 Jenny got a job back in Deniliquin – in her Country. I thought maybe we would take up farming there and we bought a small property 30km out of town. At the time, the Aboriginal community was re-evaluating where it was going and they asked Jeannette for help but she couldn't as she was working and so they asked me, and that's when I started working on community development, without knowing it – but responding to a community need.

So I started working on the edge of social development. Then my real consciousness of it happened when I took my wife's place on the Regional Council of Social Development in Deniliquin. She stepped down, Sylvia Baker resigned at the same time, and there was a need not to lose that shared vision. I've had a very challenging time since, understanding what Jenny and Sylvia's vision was, and protecting it.

I only knew of SDN through Sylvia. But I didn't know what she did there – I just knew she'd go off to these things. But this time I said I'd be interested to come. I knew of Ned who was a contemporary of my father and I wanted to visit my parents who still live in Armidale as well as drive Sylvia here. And I thought it might be useful because I'd been thrashing around all these ideas that had been coming across into my sphere. I thought, "Maybe there'll be people there who know more about this than me – all these concepts and language that I'm confronted with. Maybe there'd be some people who can give me some pointers into what this all means, rather than directly asking the people I'm engaged with." So I didn't really know what I was letting myself in for.

David's first workshop

Ok, so what have you found over the last 4 days?

I've found that it is refreshing because you could explore a different part of your identity. In working in the areas that I'm working in, it's not often that I reflect outside of the community. I do a lot inside the community – but not with people outside. I did get Sylvia to give me Ned's overview of how the workshops work, a few days before we came up – so I had an idea that if the opportunity arose I could have something to present. But I didn't realise the format meant that everyone presents. And I think that's an excellent model – to the extent that when I got around to presenting what I had, I was able to present something that I owned. While I was looking for answers, there were more questions asked of me than answers given. So yesterday I felt very confused and anxious – because I suppose people then forced me to face my own motivations. I was quite happy going along to the workshop – but this pulls me up and asks me: 'what am I doing personally'?

How did you feel about that?

Well, in the end I felt: 'OK, I know as much as everyone else here, to some extent.' But people did present me with insights that were a bit challenging – because the insights were about me rather than what I'm doing. And you don't often get to start thinking about you as the individual – that's a bit challenging and confronting. When you try to rationalise it, it doesn't rationalise! So it just lurks there. I know people have lots of techniques to work at that, but I haven't developed that perception to do that. So it's interesting – it's given me more things to think about, but I don't know if I've got the skills to deal with it. So I don't really know what to do with that. It's left me a little bit in limbo. And I suspect it will stay that way as I get back to work.

It wasn't destructive?

Oh no. It just put something else in my brain that I've got to deal with, sometime – whether it's this year, next year, five years, I don't know. Sometime I'll have to deal with it. And that's about my own personal achievements.

So do you think it's a forum you'd come back to?

Yes I think so. And I'd like to see it repeated elsewhere. So I'd like to look at a similar type of thing which brings people together to reflect and analyse on what they're doing – and at a local level on the Riverina. I can see some parts of it being very beneficial to people who are working in social development, but who don't know they are working in social development!

So what are the bits of the format that worked for you?

I'd say it's the structure – so that people can talk about where they are – and then how it fits in with the picture. But this is very confronting – this one you had to get your soul out and you can't do that when you're working with people day to day. But you can do this here – come here and come back in a year's time and do it again. Because this is away from and outside of your community at home. Here, these are people who might be able to help – be good contacts – build the contacts – and start bouncing things off. But it's not something you can do with the people you work with, and interact with, on a professional level, day to day.

What doesn't work?

I think they are very long days, but on the other hand, I'm not sure how you'd give everyone the opportunity to face all those things otherwise. So maybe everyone living in the one environment and being much more together, would, I suspect, be a better format[17]. Maybe you could have smaller groups for the very personal stuff, with someone who could be insightful, rather than bearing your soul to a whole group of 18 people. I think some people would find that very challenging to expose themselves to that big group of people when you don't know them.

Anything else you want to add about this first workshop?

I think it was interesting for me, half knowing a couple of people – well knowing Sylvia and trusting her opinion and direction. But I think I've missed out on some of the shared history – for example the 'in' conversations about theories and books. For the new people there were no references, no context for that. So initially I think some people felt out of it – not in the group – because these people have been

17   David was staying with his parents rather than staying at the pub in Uralla with a number of the other participants.

meeting for so long they've got this shared experience. And that's just a factor of what happens. But I think those people who have been in it for a long time need to be aware that's what's happening. The new people are a bit lost because they don't understand all these personal journeys that people have been on. And the other thing I'd love to see is relevance back to community. There are the theoretical and personal journeys and all this self-exploratory stuff – but then I'd also like to see how that relates to community development or social development as a process. I'd like more examples, more scenarios, techniques, 'what if I did this?'. Having learned all of this, how then can I apply it back?

Afterword

Ned Iceton – Reflections on his Life

Compiled by David Purnell

Ned was born in 1930 and raised in Gunnedah NSW. There he
learned early, especially from his mother Ailsa, the importance of community. During the Great Depression of the 1930s she supported those
in need, by taking meals to those camping out. His father Ted was a
lawyer who also assisted people who could not afford to pay during
the Depression. Ned had a younger brother Venn whom he regarded
as his best friend. He studied medicine on the understanding that it
would open the way to authentic relationships with others, and this
turned out to be the case. He went to England from 1956 to 1958 to
advance his studies, but his brother (who had also studied medicine)
was killed in Sydney in a motor-bike accident during this time, and
this led Ned to become very uncertain about his future. He eventually decided on a different path, and took a job with the Northern
Territory flying doctor service from 1958 to 1962.

Although he had rejected the Anglican Church because of a con-
tradiction between its values and behaviour, he had his own spiritual
experience of 'atonement' and connected well with Aboriginal people
in the Northern Territory when working there. He observed that both
white and black residents suffered from poor dietary options, and he
went on to study tropical medicine. His own reflection on this time
was as follows:

When I did the postgraduate Diploma in Tropical Medicine & Hygiene at Sydney University in 1962, the Professor, Robert Black, had us read about community development, among a lot of things, and I found I was immediately 'switched on'. I realised I had already begun to be a community developer while I was working as a doctor in the Territory. I had done this by raising with out-back citizens, on my daily radio session, whatever were general issues for them- for example, education services, or transport, as well as health and illness. I also had taken steps to help the staffs on missions and settlements to improve their public health arrangements and reduce the occurrence of epidemics of gastroenteritis. I came to see that lots of people can engage for real when the context is real and important, not just when they're sick. I was on the way to being a community developer.

Ned spent over a year in India, Sri Lanka and Pakistan in 1963-4 looking at public health programs and community development approaches, and he met many locals as well as UN officials from many countries. On the basis of this background he got a job in 1966 as Lecturer in Community Development at the University of New England in Armidale NSW, although he found little interest among his academic colleagues in what he was doing. As part of his transition from medicine to community development he attended experiential workshops run by Dr Maurice Marsh of the Psychology Department, and by 1970 he was running 'human relationships' workshops with Aboriginal people. He also edited a newsletter for the participants, who included Terry Widders and Ray Kelly, both of whom spoke highly of the impact of this approach and became long-term friends of Ned.

Ned connected with a group of farmers in the Inverell area (the Bannockburn Farmers) to help them deal with soil erosion and low productivity. As they shared insights and skills they developed a greater confidence in their capacity to make positive change for their families and community. For about five years Ned was involved with this group. One participant, John Ducker, explained it this way:

Ned always maintained a very unobtrusive presence. He'd sit at the back of a meeting and not enter into it at all. He'd simply observe. Then afterwards, he'd strategise the next steps with the group.

By this time Ned had devised a new style of workshop called a Social Development Practitioners Workshop, with encouragement from social worker John Russell whom he met early in the 1970s. The process was designed to enable participants to confront personal and social issues facing them. Originally the workshops were designed to support the Australian Assistance Plan (a Whitlam government initiative) under which regional councils for social development were established.

At that time, Ned described the role of the community developer as helping people identify and act upon their own priorities in their own locality. This would be done in a context of seeing both the macro and micro levels of experience and challenge. He saw it as necessary for any person to begin where they are and to work from there to achieve positive change that strengthens community life. Ned also said: "You can't be an optimal part of social development unless you're working on yourself".

Ned's life was greatly enhanced by meeting Joan and marrying her in 1972. They were both involved in Aboriginal support issues and Joan was a lecturer in education at the College of Advanced Education in Armidale. They also had mutual interests in music, landscape, cooking, and meeting people from many countries. In the Social Developers' Network (SDN) they complemented each other, with Joan taking more of a group maintenance role while Ned highlighted the analytical and social dimensions of issues raised. They travelled to USA when Joan undertook a Masters Course in 'Confluent Education', and Ned learned about meditation. He continued to practice his own form of meditation for the rest of his life. It involved concentration, pondering and insight. He would take a problem, usually a physical pain, and seek the source – usually a 'script' that was laid down in early life. He would then use current 'consciousness' to rewrite the old script.

Joan found herself out of favour with the culture of the CAE when she returned from USA, and left. Ned continued to work at the University despite many difficulties in achieving his own goals, and finally left in 1992. By that time Joan had developed cancer, and she and Ned ran in their home a meditation and support group for those dealing with cancer. When Joan died in 1993, Ned went through a lengthy period of depression. He focussed on SDN – which continued to be a source of encouragement and inspiration for him – and also took some time off for holidays. In due course he linked up with a friend Marie from the cancer group to travel and share interests, until she also died in 1998.

Within Armidale, Ned was involved in many community activities, testimony to his affirmation of the global and local fitting together. This list gives some idea of the energy he gave to local causes – City Council Safety Committee, Armidale Community Foot Patrol, Jobs Australia Armidale, Minimbah Aboriginal School, and a local Aboriginal football team. Stretching beyond Armidale was his connection with restorative justice networks, and the action learning and research association. Ned was also very generous with his own financial support of such groups over the years.

Ned also became an inveterate and valued networker, with hundreds of regular contacts all over Australia and internationally. He loved to share stimulating ideas with others and to encourage conversations both virtual and face-to-face, and arranged many stopovers to see people when travelling. The SDN workshops were the pinnacle for him, giving him the space to share more in breadth and depth his many concerns. The range of his thinking was considerable as he saw linkages across disciplines, and responded to creative community initiatives like the co-operatives movement, deep democracy, conservation projects, emotional intelligence and restorative practice. He described himself as a 'cultural therapist'.

The setting up of the Nurturing Evolutionary Development (NED) Foundation was designed to guarantee an ongoing base for social development in Australia. He envisaged an employed person working in creative ways to advance the cause, and also felt that specific local initiatives compatible with SDN's values should be supported by seeding funds.

The inspiration for the Social Developers' Network and the NED-Net Foundation is based on the following perceptions:

- That the earth and human species face a crisis of survival.

- That we all need to use our potential for inner growth for the benefit of all.

- That citizen involvement must be the primary purpose of our next evolutionary step.

- That we need to participate regularly in retreats and workshops to review our goals and objectives.

Ned brought to the workshops a life-script process. An individual is encouraged to use the following steps in sharing their life story with the group – (a) a brief description of themselves; and (b) the current state of their life, lessons learned, issues they are dealing with, and outcomes they would like. In this way, the person can include both details and reflections in their story, as a basis for inviting feedback from others. In contrast to a T-group process, this approach seems more effective in enabling people to set the agenda for how a session developed. It affirms Ned's emphasis on the importance of a culture of authentic face-to-face relationships.

SDN workshops have been sometimes confronting and disturbing for those involved. Ned's style has not always suited the expectations of others, and his strongly held convictions about the kinds of change needed for the transformation of society have been sometimes felt to be too prescriptive and not sufficiently open to other approaches. His total commitment to a particular vision of the future at times has left others feeling they could not respond in the same way and that their own life experience and lessons have not been valued sufficiently. The lack of 'formal' outcomes to workshops has been thought by some to be inadequate as guidance for their journey. At the same time, many people have expressed their gratitude for the SDN workshops and Ned's role.

Ned's path was not an easy one, with a number of significant personal losses and disappointments. But he maintained his energy as a learner, advocate, and educator.

www.ingramcontent.com/pod-product-compliance
Lightning Source LLC
Chambersburg PA
CBHW030021290326
41934CB00005B/437